Glass Bottom Boats
& Mermaid Tails

Glass Bottom Boats & Mermaid Tails

Florida's Tourist Springs

TIM HOLLIS

STACKPOLE
BOOKS

Published by
STACKPOLE BOOKS
5067 Ritter Road
Mechanicsburg, PA 17055
www.stackpolebooks.com

Printed in China

10 9 8 7 6 5 4 3 2 1

FIRST EDITION

Design by Beth Oberholtzer

Cover design by Caroline Stover

Photos by the author and illustrations from the author's collection unless otherwise noted

Front cover: *Top,* "Seeing the Under-Water Wonders in Silver Springs." *Bottom,* Weeki Wachee, "A Performance Unique in All the World."

Back cover: *Top,* "Beauties in the deep at Florida's fabulous Weeki Wachee." *Bottom,* "Florida's Silver Springs, Home of World Famous Glass Bottom Boats."

Frontispiece: This promotional photo for Weeki Wachee's *Congo Belle* riverboat hinted that mermaids could be seen along the shore. Wrong!

SILVER SPRINGS

Library of Congress Cataloging-in-Publication Data

Hollis, Tim.
    Glass bottom boats & mermaid tails : Florida's tourist springs / Tim Hollis.
        p.   cm.
    Includes bibliographical references and index.
    ISBN-13: 978-0-8117-3266-6 (pb)
    ISBN-10: 0-8117-3266-5 (pb)
    1. Springs–Florida.   2. Tourism–Florida.   I. Title: Glass bottom boats and mermaid tails. II. Title.

GB1198.3.F6H65   2006
551.49′8–dc22   2005019153

CONTENTS

INTRODUCTION
Springing into Action   1

CHAPTER ONE
Silver Springs: Fairest One of All   5

CHAPTER TWO
Silver Springs' Neighbors: Classic Cars and Cowboys   35

CHAPTER THREE
Wakulla Springs: Tarzan Meets the Creature   59

CHAPTER FOUR
Rainbow Springs: Somewhere over the Highway   75

CHAPTER FIVE
Weeki Wachee Spring: The Tail of the Mermaids   91

CHAPTER SIX
Homosassa Springs: Indian Princesses and Ivan Tors   119

CHAPTER SEVEN
And a Host of Others: The Popular and Unpopular   135

BIBLIOGRAPHY   145

INDEX   149

Springing into Action

Welcome to the latest volume in my ongoing series of nostalgic looks at the South's rich heritage of roadside tourism. Some of you may be familiar with my two previous treatments of this topic, *Dixie before Disney: 100 Years of Roadside Fun* (University Press of Mississippi, 1999) and *Florida's Miracle Strip: From Redneck Riviera to Emerald Coast* (University Press of Mississippi, 2004). If you have read the introductions to those tomes, you know how everything I write—whether tourism-related or not—stems from my own childhood memories. Since this is a different publisher, some of you may be discovering my

work for the first time, so perhaps I had better back up and reintroduce this Hollis guy to you.

I grew up just outside Birmingham, Alabama, and the South was the natural reference point for my family when vacation time rolled around each year. I'm sure that I experienced southern tourism from a slightly different perspective than all of those visitors from the North and the Midwest who came to the region on vacation, but I loved every single minute of it. My dad was a schoolteacher for forty years, and my mom did not work outside the home, so we didn't have the funds to make extended trips very often. This only served to make the ones we did take more special.

It was only natural that my dad got all the tourist literature available and then chose the most heavily advertised attractions as our earliest destinations. In the three years between the time we began taking family vacations and the time I entered first grade, we had visited four out of the "big five" Florida springs attractions. (Wakulla Springs was, as it still is, somewhat off the beaten path—and at any rate, it was not designed to have great appeal to young chil-

Left: **The author and his dad visit Rainbow Springs in 1969.** *Right:* **The same fountain is not nearly as attractive today.**

The author at age seven, horsing around at Six Gun Territory in 1970.

dren in the first place.) We revisited some of these places in future years, but the most important thing is that my dad and I saved everything possible from our trips—brochures, postcards, photographs, souvenirs—and carefully preserved it all. The fact that our family did not move around as much as some others probably helped in the preservation of this material; in fact, I still live in the same house that my family built when I was two years old, so I like to think my life has had an uncommon consistency.

Just to give you an idea about how thorough we were about saving things: When we visited Silver Springs for the first time in 1967, like most other tourists, we stopped at the International Deer Ranch. For some reason, one of the deer took an uncommon interest in my mom's dress and decided to see whether it might be good to eat. The deer had to satisfy its appetite elsewhere, but the yellow dress with toothmarks still rests in the cedar chest. Now that's a complete collection!

The 1990s saw a sudden burst of interest in roadside history and nostalgia, but most of it concentrated on the western United States, particularly the venerated Route 66. I enjoyed this burgeoning area of research but wondered why no one was doing the same for the South, with all of its quirky attractions. I had been a writer since I was seven years old, and I soon found out that I already had the resources I needed to do it myself, so that is how I fell into this particular genre. Southern tourism is not my only topic, but it is always fun to go back and revisit the subject, because it holds such nostalgic memories for me.

When Kyle Weaver of Stackpole Books first approached me about doing something on southern tourism for his company, I was a bit puzzled as to how to go on from there. It wasn't that I was lacking in material—I still have filing cabinet drawers full of stuff I haven't used yet. The problem was which aspect of tourism to revisit. Between the two of us, we came up with the commercial development of the Florida springs, because seemingly everyone who visited the Sunshine State prior to the theme-park era had to visit at least one, if not all, of them.

This book describes the promotion of the various springs as tourist destinations and the attractions that built up around them. I am no geologist, so you
will not find any explanations of the physical reasons why so many springs
gush forth throughout the Florida peninsula. The book's topic is what was
done with the springs, not how they came to exist in their natural state.

I hope this trip will be a fun and nostalgic one for you. So jump into that
car and fasten your seatbelt, and let's head for Florida. Look, there's the welcome center just up ahead on the right! We're almost to the state line, so you
know it can't be far to Silver Springs now!

CHAPTER ONE

Silver Springs
Fairest One of All

There is a story in the Florida tourism industry that many people have repeated through the years. It seems that during one presidential election year, the editor of a Florida newspaper decided he had come up with a foolproof method of predicting the winner. Supposedly he sent one of his copy boys out to the streets and highways to count the candidates' bumper stickers; the candidate with the most stickers was sure to be elected, his reasoning went.

After a while, the copy boy returned to the newspaper office with the results of his survey. The editor asked, "Well? Who's going to be elected?" The boy studied his notes and replied, "If my count is correct, the next president of the United States is going to be Silver Springs."

Now that little scene may or may not have happened in real life, but

In the 1950s, there was hardly an out-of-state automobile in Florida that did not bear a Silver Springs bumper sticker.

GINGER HALLOWELL COLLECTION

SHRINE *of* THE WATER GODS

Historical Account of
SILVER SPRINGS, FLORIDA
LOCATED AT THE HEAD OF BEAUTIFUL SILVER RIVER
by Carita Doggett Corse
AUTHOR · LECTURER · HISTORIAN

Carita Doggett Corse first published her exhaustive account of Silver Springs' prehistory, *Shrine of the Water Gods*, in the mid-1930s. It remained on sale in the gift shop for many years thereafter; this is a 1947 edition.

there is absolutely no doubt that for a large part of at least four decades, Florida's Silver Springs had not even a distant rival for its reputation as the monarch of all the state's many attractions. That position as the great-great-grandpappy of them all makes it somewhat difficult to determine just where to begin tracing its history—as, in fact, Silver Springs had beginnings.

When historian Carita Doggett Corse researched her 1930s account of Silver Springs' history, *Shrine of the Water Gods,* she elected to begin her story with the Native Americans of north-central Florida. She wrote, "Among the early Indians this region was known as Timuqua, Kingdom of the Sun, while the area around Silver Springs was a subprovince of Timuqua, called Ocali." Corse went on to elaborate for pages on the arrival of European explorers in the 1500s and all of the cultural conflicts that ensued for centuries.

FLORIDA STATE ARCHIVES COLLECTION

SILVER SPRING, OCKLAWAHA RIVER

People had known of Silver Springs since well before the Civil War, but it did not become a tourist draw until after that conflict.

The first Silver Springs tourists arrived in steamboats such as this one, which carried them on an adventuresome trip down the Ocklawaha River.

In contrast, when Richard A. Martin took a stab at Silver Springs in his 1966 book, *Eternal Spring,* he most appropriately subtitled it *Man's 10,000 Years of History at Florida's Silver Springs*. Martin chose to spend a large chunk of his text on the area's prehistory, explaining how the geography of Florida was suited to producing springs and why the fossilized remains of so many beasts have been found in the watery depths.

Each of these approaches was appropriate for its purpose, but since we are concerned here with Silver Springs' development as far as tourists are concerned, we need not overly burden ourselves with what the conquistadors and mastodons were doing. It might be argued that the first visitors to Silver Springs for purely recreational purposes began arriving in measurable numbers during the post–Civil War years. A big difference between those tourists and the carloads that would follow is that there were no automobiles to bring those first sightseers and no roads leading to Silver Springs.

No, instead, Silver Springs made its first ripples as a tourist attraction as the destination at the end of steamboat trips down the Ocklawaha River. By and large, from surviving documentation, it sounds as if the journey to get to the springs warranted more attention than the springs themselves. This was the case in particular for those well-bred souls from up North, to whom anything in the South seemed charmingly barbaric.

For example, author Harriet Beecher Stowe did not send her famous character of Uncle Tom to Silver Springs, but she made the trip herself and recorded it in her 1873 book, *Palmetto Leaves*. Poet Sidney Lanier waxed about his visit to Silver Springs in 1875: "The distinct sensation is that, although the bottom is clearly seen, and although all the objects in it are of their natural sizes undiminished by any narrowing of the visual angle, yet it and they are seen as from a great distance." Everyone who braved the eerie nighttime steamboat passages down the Ocklawaha to Silver Springs seemed to be similarly taken with the clarity of the water, which is one aspect that would remain unchanged through all of the attraction's future lives.

By the 1880s, Silver Springs was popular enough to boast its own hotel on the shore. Several people were in the business of renting small rowboats to tourists, and the traffic coming in by steamboat seemed to have no end. Things began to change when a local businessman named Ed Carmichael bought Silver Springs and started his own fleet of boats powered by internal-combustion engines, which certainly made the trip down the river faster, if less romantic. He soon put the Ocklawaha steamboat lines out of business, but the effects of World War I put Carmichael's boats into dry dock by 1919. It appeared that the popularity of Silver Springs had run its course, and the natural feature once again sat isolated in the midst of a dense forest, known only to a few local residents.

The biggest turning point in Silver Springs' history came about in 1924. That was when another Ocala businessman, William Carl Ray, started taking a second look at what could be done with such a beautiful spot. Son Bill explains what was on Ray's mind: "When my dad was a young man, he would visit Silver Springs and he'd say, 'If people just knew about this place, they'd want to come and see it.' So when he was older, he wanted to lease the property—about eighty acres around the head of the spring. (Later, the attraction took in some 4,000 acres.) The owner, Mr. Carmichael, had several different business ventures, including a boat ride. Well, every time Dad thought he had a deal with Mr. Carmichael, the price would change. So finally, after one of their meetings, Dad left and parked his car where no one could see it, and watched."

What Carl Ray saw as a result of his espionage confirmed his suspicions. Another businessman, W. C. "Shorty" Davidson, arrived and began dickering with Carmichael as well. This explained the mysteriously fluctuating price, and Ray immediately made it a point to have a private meeting with Davidson. He convinced his rival that as long as Carmichael was able to keep

William Carl Ray (seated) and W. C. "Shorty" Davidson (standing) were the business team that put Silver Springs on the Florida tourism map.

Silver Springs, Florida, "Nature's Underwater Fairyland"

Silver Springs became synonymous with glass bottom boats after Ray and Davidson took over.

them bidding against each other, neither of them was ever going to get anywhere. Ray proposed that they join forces to acquire and operate Silver Springs, and that is exactly what happened. The attraction would be a venture of the firm of Ray and Davidson for the next four decades.

It took about ten years for Ray and Davidson to upgrade Silver Springs into the type of attraction that would appeal to the necessary numbers of tourists. In the beginning, their main selling point was the Silver Springs glass bottom boat. Just how this invention came about has been the subject of much controversy over the years.

Silver Springs' official story is that the first glass bottom boat was created by one Hullam Jones in 1878, ostensibly so he could search for fallen cypress logs underneath the water's surface. For years, however, old-timers around the area claimed that Jones was actually a Hullam-come-lately, and that the original glass bottom boat was invented by Phillip Morrell, but no one was able to assign a specific date to that momentous event. They did maintain that

Linen postcards of the 1930s are known today for their completely unrealistic artificial coloring; this one is a prime example.

though the surviving example of a Hullam Jones boat might have dated back to 1878, its glass well was not added until years later.

Even historians Corse and Martin had diverging opinions when it came to glassing the history of the glass bottom boats. Martin maintained that the boats could not have been in use until the 1880s at the earliest, as none of the many pieces of writing about Silver Springs before that time mentioned any such contraptions. Corse was convinced that the first glass bottom boats did not begin their voyages until 1903, but how she arrived at this particular year is unknown. Whatever their origin, the boats were the primary asset acquired by Ray and Davidson, aside from the natural beauty of the springs themselves, and it was with this feature that they first began to tinker.

The boats that were in use in 1924 were powered by noisy outboard motors. This seemed so at odds with the serene beauty of Silver Springs that one of the pair's first actions was to have all the boats refitted with gasoline motors, which might not have helped much but at least were an improvement. In 1932, the boats were refitted yet again with electric motors, which finally produced the desired quiet, restful journey. The success of this feature can be judged by the fact that within a few years, glass bottom boats had sprouted at practically all the other Florida springs, as common as the palmetto fronds seen in the untamed wilderness.

It was not long before it became apparent that it was going to take more than just gliding along in glass bottom boats to satisfy the growing tourist clientele. Bill Ray recalls this period in his father's career: "For the first ten years they were in business, Dad got his gasoline and cigarettes out of the profits, and Shorty got his gasoline and pipe tobacco, and that was all they took out of the money. Every other penny they got was put back into building up the business and the advertising. They spent a *huge* amount of the income on the advertising. They knew the hard part was getting people to actually come to Silver Springs, because it was more remote than it is now. Once they got them

Herpetologist Ross Allen brought his snakes to Silver Springs in 1930.

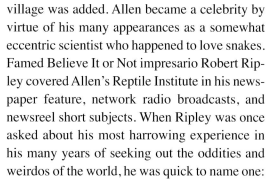

See **FLORIDA'S SILVER SPRINGS** AND **ROSS ALLEN'S REPTILE INSTITUTE**

See Giant Alligators at the Reptile Institute

Daily Program

A tour consisting of lectures and demonstrations begins on the half hour, every hour until dark. One admission is good for all day, so you may come in and out as you please.

FLORIDA ATTRACTIONS ASSOCIATION

BRING YOUR CAMERA...

there and got them out of the car, the more things there were for people to do, the more opportunities there were to get them to leave money."

What was likely the first of Silver Springs' several added attractions came about in 1930. A young man named Ross Allen had made a hobby of capturing snakes, turtles, and other reptiles from the swampy bogs around Silver Springs, and one day he approached Carl Ray with a proposition to put up an attraction of his own on the property. "Ross Allen came to see Dad," says Bill, "and he said, 'I've got about $7.50 and a carload of snakes.' So Dad said, 'I think we can work something out; you're the first honest person I've spoken with.'"

Ross Allen's Florida Reptile Institute became a mainstay of Silver Springs, enough of a success that in 1935 an entire replica Seminole Indian

village was added. Allen became a celebrity by virtue of his many appearances as a somewhat eccentric scientist who happened to love snakes. Famed Believe It or Not impresario Robert Ripley covered Allen's Reptile Institute in his newspaper feature, network radio broadcasts, and newsreel short subjects. When Ripley was once asked about his most harrowing experience in his many years of seeking out the oddities and weirdos of the world, he was quick to name one:

Ross Allen made many appearances in newsreels and television broadcasts and on radio programs, promoting both his Reptile Institute and Silver Springs in general.

Ross Allen's Seminole village gave tourists a taste of the colorful Indian culture of the Everglades.

"Being in Ross Allen's snake pit when the lights went out." I guess we'd better believe it!

The Seminoles in Ross Allen's village were not the only humans who were part of the Silver Springs show. For many years, visitors encountered an incredibly aged African American woman known only as Aunt Silla. (Some sources gave her name as Aunt Silly, but she was certainly no Lucille Ball.) Aunt Silla was the resident storyteller, her specialty being the legend behind Silver Springs' Bridal Chamber, an underwater crevasse from which issued a continuous stream of bubbles.

This legend, purported to be true, nevertheless had strong overtones of the "star-crossed lovers" theme so popular in literature and romance fiction. It involved a local girl named Bernice Mayo and her well-to-do lover, Claire Douglass. It seems that Claire's wealthy father objected to his son's love for a poor girl—sound familiar?—and the old meanie conspired to have the young man sent away on some business pretext or other. Although Claire faithfully wrote letters to his beloved, they were intercepted and destroyed by the scheming papa. Bernice obviously was not an empowered woman, because she spent all her time pining away for her sweetheart. Dying of a bro-

ken heart, she approached Aunt Silla—who, of course, was the one telling this tale—and made the old lady promise to bury her beneath the waters of Silver Springs. Aunt Silla did as she was asked, completing the task just before Claire's ill-timed return home and his visit to the springs, where he thought he was to meet his darling. Silver Springs' official printed version of the story gives the not unexpected climax:

> Suddenly he stared in horror at the sight of a woman's hand protruding from the rocks, for upon the wrist he recognized through the crystal-clear water the bracelet he had given Bernice. Straight down into the cavern he dove, and though the pressure of the deep water pained his ears terribly and his lungs felt as if they would burst, forced himself to the bottom and into the rocky crevice until he could seize Bernice's arm. . . . Then he drew himself down beside her and clasped her dead body to him in an embrace that has defied time and elements, for Aunt Silla swore that when he did so the rocks opened up to receive these unhappy lovers to the bosom of Mother Earth, then closed again over their dead bodies; and people do say their bones still repose there.

This story, whether or not plagiarized from Shakespeare, became known as "The Legend of the Bridal Chamber," and Aunt Silla delighted in telling it all the way up to the time of her own passing in the early 1950s, when she claimed to be 110 years old. Strange that Robert Ripley did not think to cover that while he was fooling around with Ross Allen's reptiles.

The brochure on the top, dating from 1934, mentions that Ray and Davidson had been operating Silver Springs for a decade. The brochure on the bottom was probably based on the Bridal Chamber legend.

Oddly, in recent years, Silver Springs has revised its own legend to claim that the Bridal Chamber is the final resting place of Indian princess Winona, who drowned herself because her father objected to her romance with the prince of a rival tribe. It can only be speculated why the Bernice Mayo–Claire Douglass tale has been supplanted by this alternate plot, which in the tourism industry is even more common and wheezy than the first one.

Another person who had a great influence on not only Silver Springs but several of the other springs as well was Newton Perry. His daughter Delee recalls how her father got hooked on Silver Springs even before the Ray and Davidson era: "My family moved from Tampa to Ocala in 1922, and my dad started looking for a place to go swimming. He found Silver Springs, which of course had not been opened as an attraction yet. It was a six-mile walk from where he lived, which is probably what made him so physically fit. When he was thirteen years old, he was the height and weight of a grown man. Well, while he was swimming out there one day, Mr. Carmichael, who owned the property, asked if he had ever taught anyone to swim. My dad said no, and Mr. Carmichael asked if he would teach his wife to swim, so that began his teaching swimming lessons."

Perry and Ross Allen became friends in high school, and the two pals often went out on joint excursions to round up more specimens for the Reptile Institute. Perry's main contribution to Silver Springs' reputation was not through Allen's snakes, but his own amazing swimming abilities.

Newsreel producers had already become aware of Silver Springs, but when Grantland Rice, creator of the popular series of *Sportlights* shorts, became acquainted with Newt Perry, it set off a whole new career for them all. Perry used his natural showmanship to stage underwater routines for several Rice films, with such titles as *Underwater Romance, Neptune's Scholars,* and *Underwater Circus.* Each of these took standard movie plots—the teenage date, classroom antics, and so forth—and made them novel again simply by the fact that they were acted out underwater. Although he probably had no idea at the time, Perry was developing techniques that he would later move north to Wakulla Springs, and still later would institute at Weeki Wachee Spring in the postwar world.

Naturally, a swimmer of Perry's ability was likely to make friends with others of similar talents, and his Hollywood connections brought him into contact with Olympic champion Johnny Weissmuller. Beginning in 1931, Weissmuller had been starring as the screen's most famous jungle resident, Tarzan, in a series of films for MGM. Three episodes had already been produced, with various lakes in the Los Angeles area substituting for Africa. After Perry, Weissmuller, and Ross Allen (who was no sluggard himself in the water)

Newton Perry performing one of his typical underwater stunts for Silver Springs in 1939.

started chumming around with each other, MGM sent the production crew to Silver Springs for the fourth episode in the series, originally titled *Tarzan in Exile* but released in 1939 as *Tarzan Finds a Son*. Silver Springs was reportedly used mainly for the underwater scenes, although it is possible that the jungle along the riverbanks may have made a few appearances as well. By the time the fifth and sixth Tarzan films were in production, Perry had moved to Wakulla Springs as general manager, and MGM followed him there.

The jungle habitat of central Florida became an attraction at Silver Springs in its own right, apart from Tarzan's swinging adventures. At some point during the 1930s, a promoter named Colonel Tooey approached Ray and Davidson with another idea. (And in case you are wondering, Colonel was his first name, not a title, honorary or otherwise.) Tooey's wanted to expand Silver Springs' coverage area beyond the head of the springs and take people on a speedboat jungle cruise down the Silver River. This was a more modern approach to the idea

Tourists went bananas over the rhesus monkeys in Colonel Tooey's Jungle Cruise ride.

begun when the steamboats of yore brought venturesome tourists to Silver Springs, and it was another hit.

To enhance the jungle atmosphere, Tooey imported some rhesus monkeys and set up a residence for them on one of the islands in the middle of the river. More of a showman than a zoologist, Tooey was unaware that monkeys are excellent swimmers—it has been speculated that they instinctively realize that alligators get the slow ones—and within hours, the new Jungle Cruise attractions had abandoned their enforced solitude and escaped to the real-life jungle on shore. Colonies of their descendants populated Silver Springs' forests for many decades to come. (Some historians, including Richard Martin, have claimed that the monkeys escaped from the Tarzan film sets, but others have pointed out that the ape man's screen companions were chimps, not rhesus monkeys.)

World War II hurt the tourism industry, since the rationing of gasoline and rubber, along with all of the other wartime hardships, effectively stopped tourists from making pleasure trips for the duration. Silver Springs did manage to hang on, even as other attractions closed their doors until the fighting was over. Bill Ray recalls that during the war, Colonel Tooey had his Jungle Cruise boat motors converted from gasoline to propane, and in one amusing way the war crossed over with his attraction: "A guy who worked for Colonel

Silver Springs had been popular enough before World War II, but in the years that followed, it would become nearly invincible as a tourist hot spot.

Tooey was drafted, and while he was in the army camp, Tooey called out there and said, 'This is Colonel Tooey at Ocala, and I wondered how So-and-So is doing.' Well, when the camp heard it was Colonel Tooey calling, the guy said all of a sudden things got a lot better for him!"

If Ray and Davidson thought Silver Springs was a hot spot before the war, they hadn't seen anything to compare with what happened once the baby boom started and hundreds of thousands of families made Florida their vacation destination. Silver Springs' more-than-gigantic reputation was partly due to the success of its marketing program, but conversely, the marketing program was a hit because of Silver Springs' immediate name recognition. The amount of its advertising in the late 1940s and early 1950s would be inconceivable to a tourist attraction of comparable size today. Silver Springs brochures were printed in quantities of seven million at one time; its postcards were printed not only in English, but also in German, Portuguese, and Spanish.

Bill Ray was serving as public-relations manager during this period and got to see firsthand the all-out promotional blitz his dad's attraction warranted. He recalls the time they received a shipment of new brochures, only to find that someone at the printing company had made a behemoth booboo. The line that read "Alcoholic beverages are not permitted at Silver Springs" had inadvertently omitted one important word: "not." "That was like leaving a word out of one of the Ten Commandments," says Ray, who had to have the entire run shipped back to the pathetic printer. Examples of those brochures

Top: **This pose by model Jackie Bingham was featured on countless Silver Springs brochures and souvenirs. During this period, Silver Springs' marketing was so huge that brochures had to be printed in quantities of seven million at a time.** *Bottom:* **Public-relations manager Bill Ray was constantly posing as a typical camera-toting tourist for shots such as the one on this brochure. "I had the most famous back in the country," he comments.**

exist today, with a red asterisk denoting the word *not,* printed hastily in the bottom margin.

Silver Springs promoted itself in any tourist medium possible but was especially known for its billboards. At an outdoor advertising show, a southern attraction owner reportedly stated, "Give me a four-by-eight board and a can of red paint, and I can get a Yankee to do anything." This was the philosophy that drove the entire southern tourism industry, which thrived on those visitors from the North who made the long drive to the land of sand and sunshine.

"At one time, we had billboards all the way to Maine," says Bill Ray. "We would have a billboard at each state line: 'As you're leaving Maine (or whatever), be sure to see Florida's Silver Springs.' We would have miniature billboards made for people who had model train sets."

Another popular promotional piece was the Silver Springs mileage meter. These meters were placed in the lobbies of motels across the eastern half of the country. Requiring a staggering amount of work, each meter had to have a custom-typewritten paper on its rotating drumhead, calculating the distance

GINGER HALLOWELL COLLECTION

The appropriate place names and mileages to Silver Springs were filled in on these photos, which then became billboards stretching from Maine to Florida.

In the 1950s, Silver Springs' entrance sported this eye-catching space-age design.

VAL VALENTINE COLLECTION

to Silver Springs from wherever the meter was going to be placed. At first Silver Springs provided the meters to motels free of charge. According to Ray: "We used to give away the mileage meters, and people were very careless and would break them. Finally we had the businesses pay for the meters, and for some reason the breakage stopped immediately!"

Besides the promotions along the side of the road, another thing that kept Silver Springs' marketing department busy was the distribution of photo features to major magazines and newspaper wire services. It was Silver Springs' good fortune that in the early 1950s, a most photogenic, not to mention athletic, young lady named Ginger Stanley Hallowell came to work for them.

Hallowell had originally been discovered by Newt Perry, who by that time had carved out his own watery kingdom at Weeki Wachee Spring. She was the Ocala contestant in a beauty pageant where one of the Weeki Wachee mermaids was also competing, and Perry offered her a job as one of his performers. She soon moved over to Silver Springs as a swimmer and model, initially working only on weekends while maintaining her Weeki Wachee job during the week.

The blonder-than-blond Hallowell became the undisputed star of Silver Springs' underwater photo shoots. Resident photographer Bruce Mozert had long been experimenting with ways to improve the always tricky art of photographing

Ginger Stanley Hallowell was Silver Springs' busiest underwater model during the 1950s. She recalls that photographer Bruce Mozert had to snap the "target" shot at the exact moment she released the arrow, before it floated to the water's surface.

GINGER HALLOWELL COLLECTION

This beautiful promenade replaced the Silver Springs buildings that were destroyed in the June 1955 fire.

beneath the surface, and he reached something of a peak during his years of shooting Hallowell in every conceivable underwater situation. When additional actors were needed, publicity man Ricou Browning would fill in for any male roles that were needed; brunette secretary Dee Dee Adams could be counted on for additional female scenery.

Mozert became another huge part of Silver Springs' legend during this era, although he was not on public display personally. Always on the lookout for new publicity, Mozert even found opportunity in disaster. In June 1955, a fire consumed all the buildings housing Silver Springs' administrative offices, gift shops, and restaurant. Was Mozert downhearted? No, he went up in a small airplane and shot photos of the burning buildings, which he then sold as souvenirs once his photo shop reopened. A true opportunist!

Even though Johnny Weissmuller had long since hung up his Tarzan loincloth, the motion-picture studios kept flocking to Silver Springs in the late

1940s and 1950s. Most of the classic film version of *The Yearling* (1949) was shot on location at Silver Springs, and Gary Cooper said "yup" to Ocala when he was there for the filming of *Distant Drums* (1951). Esther Williams, whose fame as a swimming champ rivaled that of Weissmuller, dove into Silver Springs for the 1955 feature *Jupiter's Darling*, but with an unusual twist. Although one would not expect an expert like

Silver Springs' publicity man Ricou Browning suits up for one of his three appearances as the Creature from the Black Lagoon.

SILVER SPRINGS COLLECTION

Santa Creature is coming to town? Ginger Stanley Hallowell and Ricou Browning were often teamed for shots such as this holiday-themed one.

Williams to require a double, Ginger Stanley Hallowell had to substitute for her in some of the underwater sequences. It seems that Williams was nursing a perforated eardrum at the time, limiting her submersions. In addition, much of the action took place at greater depths than she was accustomed to in her competitive swimming background.

Besides their many joint photo shoots, Hallowell and Ricou Browning were teamed again for another motion-picture venture. In 1953, Browning had appeared as the gruesome gill man who was the title character of *The Creature from the Black*

Silver Springs' publicity department sent out "photo comic strips" such as this one to newspapers all over the country. A husband (Ricou Browning) is surprised when a beautiful girl (Ginger Stanley Hallowell) emerges from his TV screen, but his wife (Dee Dee Adams) doesn't think so much of it and gives the philandering fink a piece of her mind.

Lagoon. Inasmuch as Browning was employed by Wakulla Springs at the time, all of his sequences for that movie were filmed at the location near Tallahassee; Hallowell did the stunt swimming for leading lady Julia Adams. By the time the inevitable sequel, *Revenge of the Creature,* was filmed in 1955, both Browning and Hallowell were firmly entrenched at Silver Springs, so the underwater action took place there instead, with additional scenes shot at Marineland, near St. Augustine. Browning menaced society again for a third installment, *The Creature Walks among Us* (1956), which split its underwater filming between Silver Springs and Wakulla Springs.

A major event was the 1955 premiere of Jane Russell's movie *Underwater!* which had an effect that no one expected. A publicity man managed to get up-and-coming starlet Jayne Mansfield to the event, and she wore a swimsuit that became transparent when wet. The photographers on hand to cover the premiere were suddenly taking more photos of Mansfield than of the stars of the movie, for some reason, and by the time they all returned to Hollywood, Mansfield was a celebrity. That's show biz!

As a result of Silver Springs' newly bulging muscle in the tourism world, more add-on attractions were attached to the property in the 1950s. One of these was the idea of CBS radio and television host Tommy Bartlett, who had already made a second career for himself in the tourism-happy world of the Wisconsin Dells. Bartlett had been busy putting on water ski shows up at the Dells—presumably for those who could not get to Florida's Cypress Gardens to see them—but he had also found himself spending

Tommy Bartlett reportedly got the idea for his Deer Ranch at Silver Springs from a similar establishment in the Wisconsin Dells.

This impressive Deer Ranch folder shows the many activities available.

more and more time at a local deer ranch that doubled as a petting zoo. Bartlett had in mind that tourists might fawn over a similar attraction in Florida, so after some brief negotiations, Tommy Bartlett's International Deer Ranch opened in a corner of Silver Springs' property in 1954.

Besides the deer that were the main attraction at the ranch, numerous other animals were on display, courtesy of the I.Q. Zoo park in Hot Springs, Arkansas. Drumming ducks, fortune-telling chickens, kissing bunnies, and dancing chickens were all part of the menagerie. Besides these talented furry and feathered performers, the Bartlett Deer Ranch was also perhaps one of the most artistic galleries in Florida tourism.

This was due mainly to the presence of Vincent "Val" Valentine, a commercial artist whose career went back to the famed Max Fleischer animated cartoon studio in Miami in the late 1930s and early 1940s. Valentine created countless set pieces for the Bartlett Deer Ranch, some of which definitely showed the influence of his animation background. One of Valentine's most prominent photo ops was Santa's South Pole, a candy-striped cane topped by a comical cartoon penguin. Continuing the somewhat tenuous Christmas

These performing animal displays definitely show the influence of artist Val Valentine's background as a cartoon animator.

theme, visitors to the main Silver Springs property could be transported to Bartlett's via a replica of St. Nick's sleigh and reindeer, another masterful Valentine creation.

Tommy Bartlett visits with kids around Val Valentine's Santa's South Pole creation. Tourists were shuttled between Silver Springs and the Deer Ranch in a replica of St. Nick's sleigh and reindeer.

Another artist who took up residence at Silver Springs around the same time was Paul Cunningham, whose approach differed greatly in both style and subject matter. Cunningham's Prince of Peace Memorial was described thus:

It is a series of beautifully hand-carved scenes from the life of Christ, presented in the most interesting manner possible. Entrance to the Memorial is through the Bell Tower and artist's studio. In the beautiful garden beyond are the little chapels, each containing a 3-dimensional scene from the Greatest Life ever lived. The superbly lighted scenes in full color, with a background of rich carillonic bell music, bring to life in startling realism the dramatic events in Christ's life.

Yes, it does sound as if a few years later the Christus Gardens attraction in Gatlinburg, Tennessee, might have borrowed a concept or two from Silver Springs, but Cunningham's memorial was well capable of standing on its own merits. Little biographical data about Cunningham

The Prince of Peace Memorial was a reflective alternative to the rest of the Silver Springs property. Paul Cunningham was the woodcarver responsible for the sacred scenes.

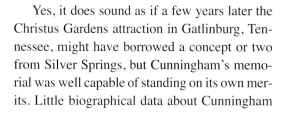

The hand-carved scenes at the Prince of Peace Memorial were displayed in miniature chapels such as this one.

was documented, except that he began his woodcarving career in Washington, D.C., and supposedly carved his first scene from the wood of an old former pulpit. The Geppetto of the Gospels strove to make his Prince of Peace Memorial a quiet and reflective alternative to all the commercialism on the rest of the property. Oh, and

See **FLORIDA'S**
SILVER SPRINGS
FROM
PARADISE PARK
FOR COLORED PEOPLE

...NG GLASS BOTTOMED BOAT RIDE
...WATERS OF SILVER SPRINGS

KEN BRESLAUER COLLECTION

don't forget to pass the collection plate: Adults paid 50 cents to see the exhibit, while kids were charged only two bits.

In those days, especially in the South, what one could do and where one could go was determined in no small part by what color one's skin happened to be. Silver Springs

Unfortunately, not everyone was welcomed at Silver Springs with open arms, so Paradise Park opened in 1949 as an alternative.

Silver Springs made the cover of Standard Oil's 1959 map of Florida.

employed numerous African American boat drivers, but their fellow citizens were not allowed as passengers. (Aunt Silla undoubtedly would have run into similar discrimination had she wished to revisit the Bridal Chamber on one of the glass bottom boats.) Whether or not they agreed with the idea of segregation, Ray and Davidson were not about to let this flaw in social mores take away potential income, so in 1949 they opened a branch attraction known as Paradise Park, promoted in its brochures as "Silver Springs for Colored People."

Other than this stipulation, Paradise Park offered most of the same opportunities as its more well-publicized big brother. Glass bottom boats made the same trip over the water, with the same

This handy-dandy layout shows how all of Silver Springs' many attractions were laid out in relation to each other.

For a period of time, Silver Springs had hidden speakers in the trees, and chimes concerts were given at regular intervals.

drivers in charge, and Ross Allen would pick up his snakes and slither over to Paradise Park to perform his venom-milking demonstrations. As times and attitudes changed, the need for Paradise Park thankfully grew obsolete, and it was closed as a "separate but equal" attraction around 1956, in time for visitors of all races and creeds to enjoy the Bartlett Deer Ranch and the Prince of Peace Memorial.

By the 1960s, Silver Springs was a household word. This was the era of the comedy record, and Bob Corley, a cornball comic from Macon, Georgia, had a hit with his 45-rpm single "Number One Street," which described his family vacation to Florida along U.S. Highway 1. (In style and approach, and being recorded in front of a live audience, the routine owed

Motel rooms all over Florida featured Silver Springs photos as decorations.

Model Betty Frazee looks as if she's thinking, "Mozert, if you don't hurry up and snap the photo, I'm about to drown."

much to Andy Griffith's earlier smash, "What It Was Was Football.") Corley could not let any description of Florida go by without a comment on Ocala's most famous sight:

> We kept seein' these billboards that said, "See Silver Springs through Our Glass Bottoms." Nothin' would do but that we had ta go. So we rid over the clearest water while the boat driver named off all the springs. They all had purty names like the Fairy Castul an' the Bridal Chamber—all 'cept one, and hit wuz called the Bottomless Pit. Well, the boat driver said, 'Friends, yo're lookin' into the Bottomless Pit, a spring so deep that no human eye kin see to the bottom.' Hit upset me when he said that, 'cause I wuz a-lookin' clear to the bottom at the time. And you know whut wuz down ther? Hit wuz a sign that said SEE ROCK CITY.

This 1960 brochure was one of the last produced before ABC-Paramount bought out Ray and Davidson.

FLORIDA'S **Silver Springs**

FREE FLORIDA MAP INSIDE

NATURE'S UNDERWATER FAIRYLAND

There were more similarities between Silver Springs and Rock City than just a comedian's punch line, especially in the way the two southern tourism titans promoted themselves along the nation's highways. Both enlisted the help of countless motels, restaurants, and service stations in promoting their wonders. In addition to the customized mileage meters, a line of which Rock City also distributed, there were also Silver Springs doormats for motel rooms and framed photos that hung on the walls. Bill Ray remembers that some of these photos were more popular than others. Views of the glass bottom boats were welcome sights, and the cute deer at the Bartlett ranch were proven crowd pleasers, but for some reason many people objected to having a giant color image of Ross Allen's snakes hanging over their motel bed or restaurant table.

Those few people who got creeped out by Allen's creepy crawlers had little influence on Silver Springs' success during the 1960s. Producer Ivan Tors used the clarity of the water for the underwater scenes of his syndicated television series *Sea Hunt*, starring Lloyd Bridges. Former Creature from the

Florida's **SILVER SPRINGS**

Explore the indescribable beauty of the world's largest group of crystal clear springs through the magic of world famous glass bottom boats. See more than 35 varieties of fish and 100 varieties of colorful plant life in 14 excitingly different spring groups. Admission to the 100 acre magnificently landscaped park and parking is all free. Cafeteria on grounds — Food by Morrison's

The main spring basin glows like a huge jewel in the warm Florida sun.

Enjoy the splendor of the 100 acre landscaped park that borders the tranquil Silver River.

Walk eight feet under water. . . . Take never-to-be-forgotten pictures in air-conditioned aquatorium. . . . See spectacular specimens of plant and marine life through the sparkling crystal clear water.

UNDERWATER MOTION PICTURE CAPITAL OF THE WORLD

Thrill to the untamed fury of huge alligators at the Ross Allen Reptile Institute.

A colony of wild "Tarzan" monkeys frolic in the dense tropical jungle along the Silver River and are thrown bits of food by the Captain of the Jungle Cruise.

CAMPING GROUND OF THE SEMINOLE INDIANS

Rain or shine you can enjoy every attraction any day of the year.
Glass Bottom Boats operate continuously from 8:30 A.M. daily.

Marvel at thousands of fish and many varieties of beautiful plant life in fourteen sparkling springs through the magic of World Famous Glass Bottom Boats.

You can pet and hand feed more than 300 tame deer from all over the world at the International Deer Ranch.

A good example of the new, spiffy brochure style used after the ABC-Paramount buyout.

ABC had this "waterfall" entrance constructed to replace the old Jetsons-style one. Since then, the entrance has been moved several hundred yards to the west, and the second photo shows the former entrance as it appears today.

Black Lagoon Ricou Browning stood in for the villains, who received a sound underwater thrashing in most episodes. One 1960s film that most people probably thought was about Silver Springs was Doris Day's *The Glass Bottom Boat* (1966). Instead of Florida, it was set off the coast of California, proving that those boats, be they invented by Phillip Morrell or Hullam Jones, had certainly spread to the far corners of the tourist world.

In 1962, the ABC-Paramount broadcasting and movie-theater conglomerate came knocking at Silver Springs' ticket window. The company had bought longtime Florida staple Weeki Wachee Spring a few years earlier. Ray and Davidson sold out to ABC and quit their association with the springs forever, though Carl Ray's oldest son, Carl Jr., or "Buck," remained on staff for a time as a consultant to ease the transition.

DELEE PERRY COLLECTION

Delee Perry, daughter of Silver Springs pioneer promoter Newt Perry, returned to her dad's alma mater for some publicity work in 1970.

ABC did not make any major changes to the way things had been done, except for pumping more money into the attraction. A handsome new entrance sign was constructed, with a large glass bottom boat model topping

Model Kitty Carr and the fawns from the International Deer Ranch compete to see who can look the cutest.

a cascading waterfall. One rather silent change occurred within a year or two of the ABC purchase: Since Tommy Bartlett was an established CBS personality, his name soon disappeared from his antlered friends' display. In future publicity, it would be known simply as the International Deer Ranch.

While such outside events as the construction of Interstate 75 down Florida's midsection and the opening of Walt Disney World at Orlando in 1971 had sometimes devastating repercussions for the rest of the state's tourist industry, Silver Springs remained hale and hearty. It was no longer the primary destination that it had once been, but people kept coming nonetheless. In time, parent company ABC began buying out the contracts of the various peripheral concessionaires who had long been associated with the springs, including Ross Allen's Reptile Institute and the International Deer Ranch. Rather than sell the Prince of Peace Memorial, Paul Cunningham packed up his carvings and took them on tour to other parts of the country; at last report, they were on display at a religious retreat somewhere in the Carolinas. Once ABC gained control of the other attractions, it tended to close and demolish them. Both the reptiles and the deer were gone by 1975 or thereabouts.

In 1984, ABC sold Silver Springs and Weeki Wachee to Florida Leisure Attractions, and this entity in turn sold Silver Springs to the state of Florida in 1993. Florida Leisure continued operating both parks under a lease agreement, until it unloaded the floundering Weeki Wachee in 1999. At the dawn of the twenty-first century, Silver Springs was positioning itself as primarily a wildlife park, with the glass bottom boats being one of the few vestiges that remained from its long Ray and Davidson period. One of the last remaining 1930s features, the venerable Jungle Cruise, was replaced with a more educational voyage that incorporated the area's history into its itinerary — including a replica movie set representing that major aspect of Silver Springs' past.

Today there are probably few people who travel to Florida expressly to see Silver Springs, but it remains a vital link between the attractions of the past and today's high-tech theme parks. With the demise of so many other former tourist destinations that were its contemporaries, it is comforting to know that there will likely always be a Silver Springs, where those glass bottom boats will continue helping people see clearly into another world beneath the water.

CHAPTER TWO

Silver Springs' Neighbors

Classic Cars and Cowboys

As if one even needed a measure of Silver Springs' success, it can be gauged by the sheer number of other attractions that grew up in its immediate vicinity to siphon some of the tourist traffic. Another whole tourism world existed that did not intrude on Silver Springs' property but cashed in on the vacationing families headed for the attraction.

Since there was little development on Florida State Highway 40 east of Silver Springs, most of the tie-in businesses clustered along the road beginning at the attraction's entrance gate and continuing for at least a couple miles west, in the direction of Ocala. In fact, Highway 40 was eventually named Silver Springs Boulevard, so there was no mistaking where it led. It is not surprising that the first ancillary businesses to hook onto Silver Springs' silver lining were tourist cottages (and later, motels). Silver Springs provided no facilities for overnight stays, and these entrepreneurs became the first to find a need and fill it.

Even before the rise of tourist courts, there were tourist homes, which were much like boardinghouses but catered to temporary visitors instead of permanent residents. In the early 1930s, a tourist home was one of the few lodging choices available for visitors to the Silver Springs area, but much work needed to be done to ensure cooperation among all the parties. This is illustrated by an incident that brought together two of the biggest giants of southern tourism.

In 1932, Chattanooga businessman Garnet Carter, who had already made a name for himself by popularizing a franchised chain of miniature golf courses, was preparing to open an attraction high atop Lookout Mountain in Georgia. Carter's park was to be known as Rock City Gardens, and he had high hopes of serving thousands of tourists on their way from the North to Florida and back. To seek advice on the still-developing southern tourism industry, Carter made a trip to Silver Springs to consult with Shorty Davidson.

Carter took a room at one of the tourist homes near Silver Springs, and during breakfast, he decided to get an idea of how the attraction was perceived locally. He asked the lady host what she thought about Silver Springs, and he was surprised when she nonchalantly replied, "It's not so much. There are springs like that all over Florida." Upon meeting with Davidson, Carter related the story and asked how Silver Springs dealt with such blasé people. Davidson reportedly leaned back in his chair and said, "Well, Garnet, I just pray for them."

Over the next few years, both Silver Springs and Rock City found numerous ways to win the support of tourist facilities, and a more mutual respect developed. Silver Springs' brochures from the pre–World War II era do not mention the availability—or lack—of nearby lodging, but by the late 1940s, this emerging trend was beginning to be noted in the attraction's advertising. One promotional piece from 1949 gives this update on the situation:

> Should you decide to spend the night or longer at Silver Springs, you have your choice of five hotel or cabin courts. None are operated by or are under the control of Ray and Davidson, co-operators of Silver Springs's recreation area, but all are recommended. None is equipped for housekeeping. All are within walking distance of the springs, either down the main highway or along trails through the forest. Reservation is advisable, especially on weekends, and from a week to ten days in advance.

Now that the local accommodations' owners had learned that it was good business to be tied in with Silver Springs, some of them reversed Garnet Carter's earlier tourist home experience to a ridiculous extent. Much of the Florida tourism industry's reputation had been built on the concept of northerners arriving to spend the entire winter in the Sunshine State, and Ray and Davidson felt that they had to address this trend in the same breath as their endorsement of the local facilities:

> Although hotel or cabin courts near Silver Springs invite you to stay through any season, you should understand that Silver Springs and its indescribable underwater life can be seen and enjoyed in a minimum of 90 minutes; that all of its many and varied wonders can be covered in a maximum of four hours.

Regardless of how long or short the guests' stay might have been, over the next few years it seemed there was enough business for everyone. Another brochure from 1955 announced that nearly twenty-five hundred hotel and motel rooms were available in the Silver Springs area, quite a jump from the five cabin courts mentioned just six years earlier.

This number of rooms is especially impressive considering the typical size of a motel in those days. The Swim-In Court, for example, advertised itself as "a beautiful 24-unit court with central hot water heat and individual air conditioning, featuring full tile baths and a 25 x 50 private tile swimming pool with filtered fresh water for guest use." Similarly, the Spring Side Motel, which creatively used a seahorse as the first S in its logo, had twenty-eight units and promoted a "free TV in every room."

The Sun Plaza Motel, within walking distance of Silver Springs, was a giant among motels with forty-eight units. It also sported a spacious front lawn with concrete picnic tables, plus a playground for the kids. In addition to all the usual amenities, Cordrey's Tourist Court offered "gift boxes of tree ripened fruit and fresh citrus juices." Like many Florida businesses, the motels charged higher rates during the winter months, topping out at $5 in 1950. So as not to frighten away potential business, Cordrey's noted that these extravagant rates were reduced in the summer.

CORDREY'S TOURIST COURT — Two Blocks from Heart of City
On Route 40 — OCALA, FLA. — (On Silver Springs Blvd.)

The motel that snagged the choicest location was the Shalimar Motor Court, which had the good fortune of being directly across Highway 40 from the Silver Springs parking lot. So prime was this piece of real estate that in 1961, the Shalimar was bought out by Holiday Inn. That hotel giant continues to operate in the same spot today, although the Shalimar's original space-age architecture is no longer to be seen.

Cordrey's Tourist Court, a relic of the days before true motels, and the later Spring Side Motel, which certainly had a logo that was fitting for its area, both were among the many establishments catering to those who came to see the wonders of Silver Springs.

The Sun Plaza Motel was located across the street and within walking distance of Silver Springs' entrance. Remarkably, its original signage has been preserved, as well as some of the 1950s picnic tables on the front lawn.

While all the motels were fighting over who was to be king of the road, local restaurants kept all the combatants well fed. The Candle Glow Inn hoped to warm the insides of hungry travelers. The 1890 Beef House offered Victorian-themed dining areas. The Blue Bird Restaurant was a favorite nesting place, and the Plantation Pancake Inn served up breakfast for those who had enough Yankee dollahs. Following in the wake of Holiday Inn, many other motel chains linked themselves with Silver Springs, and every one seemed to have its own adjoining restaurant: Howard Johnson's, Ramada Inn, Travelodge, and Horne's (similar to Stuckey's but with a bright yellow roof) were among these gentle giants.

One of the most well-known restaurants was the Brahma (and that's no bull), whose bar area featured an impressive mural depicting the highways and principal sights of central Florida. This was yet another creation by Silver Springs' extraordinary commercial artist Val Valentine, whose work was seen by anyone visiting the state's attractions during that period.

Valentine was responsible for the artwork seen on the brochures for one of the most obscure and short-lived ventures in the area, the Silver Springs U-Drive-It Railroad. This complex, which aspired to be a theme park without quite making it, was just west of Silver Springs on Highway 40. Its primary feature—actually, its only feature—was a miniature diesel locomotive that took passengers through a miniaturized landscape. Everything, including the train itself, was scaled to one-fifth actual size.

The novelty was that would-be Casey Joneses could rent the train and drive it personally, with an instructor

SEE SILVER SPRINGS

SILVER SPRINGS FLORIDA

Holiday Inn

AT ENTRANCE TO SILVER SPRINGS

WITHIN EASY WALKING DISTANCE TO GLASS-BOTTOM BOATS AND OTHER ATTRACTIONS

YOUR HOST FROM COAST TO COAST®

The Shalimar Motor Court snagged a prime location directly across the street from Silver Springs. In 1961, the motel was bought by Holiday Inn; notice that the giant chain left the original architecture intact.

Silver Springs' resident artist Val Valentine painted this mural of central Florida for the bar area of the Brahma Restaurant.

looking over their shoulders. For obvious reasons, children younger than eight years old were discouraged from this budding career as an engineer. Along this line of thinking, the railroad's brochures contained a statement that might not have been the most accurate comparison: "Our equipment is kept as clean as your family automobile." For families traveling with small children, that probably wasn't saying much.

The U-Drive-It Railroad was derailed not long after its opening, unable to draw sufficient business away from all the other fun surrounding Silver Springs. Still, its Val Valentine–designed brochure was certainly one of the most artistic to be found in the area, one of the few that exclusively featured artwork of the attraction and no actual photos showing the property.

The Silver Springs U-Drive-It Railroad gave anyone a chance to be an engineer, be it a young kid, an old geezer, or, to judge from this artwork, a bathing beauty.

The Carriage Cavalcade rattled into town in 1953.

Valentine's work was also on display at another attraction that placed itself across from Silver Springs, rubbing elbows with the Shalimar Motor Lodge/Holiday Inn. This was the Carriage Cavalcade, a museum that opened in 1953 to display the automobiles and other means of transportation from the previous half century.

Needless to say, even at that time, one could not accumulate such a collection of vintage vehicles unless one had a lot of spare change, and the owners of the Carriage Cavalcade's inventory were certainly well oiled. Sam and Vernon Jarvis were responsible for Florida's Jarvis Oil Company, so it seems quite fitting that they chose to spend their extra bucks on the cars that had made their company successful.

Early publicity for the Carriage Cavalcade tried to make it clear that there was more to the attraction than just looking at a bunch of parked cars. Many of the vehicles were displayed in diorama settings that attempted to re-create each appropriate era, with mannequins garbed in whatever clothing suited the occasion. There was indeed something for everyone. As the brochure exclaimed:

> The kids will thrill at the sight of the huge horse drawn fire engine hitched to four big lifelike white horses, and the real western Concord stage coach is bound to catch

The building that housed the Carriage Cavalcade was ordinary to look at; the real show was on the inside (and on the front lawn).

This romantic couple appears to have driven in from the nostalgic past to promote the Carriage Cavalcade.

their eye. The older folks will spend many happy moments reminiscing among the well loved and remembered carriages and cars.

Whereas visitors to the Bartlett Deer Ranch were shuttled back and forth in a replica of Santa's sleigh, the Carriage Cavalcade also found novel ways to bring in pedestrians. A driver would make the rounds of the Silver Springs property in an antique car, picking up anyone who wanted to hitchhike over to the museum. Later, the artistic talents of Val Valentine were put to use, and he fashioned an eccentric streetcar modeled after the 1920s comic-strip con-

VAL VALENTINE COLLECTION

On the Carriage Cavalcade's front lawn, passengers could hitch a ride on the Toonerville Trolley of comic strip fame to shuttle back and forth to Silver Springs. A typically whimsical Val Valentine display lacks only a couple of tourists' heads to make it complete.

Around 1963, the Carriage Cavalcade became the Early American Museum, and the exterior of the building was jazzed up with huge electric signage.

veyance known as the Toonerville Trolley. This had the advantage of seating more passengers than a standard auto could hold. Valentine also plied his paintbrush on some displays for the Carriage Cavalcade's front lawn, including a funny flivver with whirling wheels.

After operating basically unchanged for its first decade, the Carriage Cavalcade found that it needed to keep up with the times as the 1960s got under way. For a brief period around 1963, the name of the attraction became Cavalcadia, which made no sense to anyone and most tourists probably could not even pronounce. ("Daddy, what's that sign say?" "Oh, it says Cavel— —Cacad— — Calava— —eh, we don't want to stop there anyway!") Before long, wiser heads had prevailed, and the building became known as the Early American Museum, complete with flashier electrical signage to increase its roadside presence.

With its new theme, the Early American Museum was able to stray off the beaten path of antique autos and visit other aspects of the nation's collective nostalgia. One of its best-remembered displays was an entire room devoted to a miniature circus,

Children visiting the Early American Museum were especially fascinated by the miniature circus, which came to life when activated by a series of buttons.

crafted with meticulous detail. As visitors prom-
enaded around the little big top, they could acti-
vate buttons that brought one or another part of
the scene to life. Other rooms displayed vintage
clothing—probably stemming from the costumes
that had to be accumulated for the mannequins—
and dolls and toys from the early years of the
century. It has been pointed out elsewhere that
the most ironic aspect of the whole concept is

**As a symbol of the Early American Museum's range from the past to the future,
this replica rocket ship stood in the parking lot. It survives today at a VFW lodge
north of Silver Springs.**

The former museum building later served as an American Precision Industries manufacturing plant but today sits mostly unused. In an overgrown section of the parking lot, the concrete supports for the long-gone rocket ship can still be seen.

that today, the automobiles and clothing and toys of 1963 are museum pieces and expensive collectibles, proving that while the Early American Museum's displays might have stood still, time does not.

Perhaps in recognition of this fact, by the end of the 1960s, the Early American Museum tour climaxed in a visit to a full-size space capsule. In the parking lot next to the building, a giant replica of a U.S. missile or rocket stood at attention.

One could sell nostalgia for only so long, though, and reportedly it was around 1977 that the Jarvis family sold out their collection to Silver Springs proper—or actually to ABC, then owner of the attraction. Just what happened to the museum after that is somewhat hazy, as no one really cared enough to keep up with it at the time. It does seem to be an established fact that the collection of antiques—including the vehicles, toys, and vintage clothing—was auctioned off in 1983. The miniature circus reportedly was dismantled, and various pieces of the scene went home with many different individuals. The missile from the parking lot ended up being launched into a new orbit north of town, where to this day it still stands in front of a Veterans of Foreign Wars (VFW) lodge.

The museum building was adapted for much more mundane use, including serving as a manufacturing plant for American Precision Industries. At last report, it was once again sitting vacant, with several of the original nostalgic lamp posts still adorning the overgrown parking lot. In a clump of subtropical Florida foliage sits a strange shape made up of four tapering concrete posts, as well as a tall concrete post on which fading red and white stripes can barely be seen. People wonder what this strange object is, not realizing it represents all that is left of the supports for the missile that has long since blasted off.

Other folks were not as interested in horseless carriages as they were in the horses the automobile replaced—and for tourists looking for relics of an even more bygone day than the turn of the century, the Silver Springs neighborhood also had something to offer them.

On the morning of May 24, 1962, a press conference was held at the offices of the Ocala Chamber of Commerce. R. B. Coburn, president of Western Heritage U.S.A. Corporation, made the announcement that within a year, his company would be opening a two hundred–acre Western theme park on property fronting State Highway 40. No name was given for the new development, but no one questioned its legitimacy, as Coburn was already an old cowhand at this game by that time.

Coburn's tourism career began in Orangeburg, South Carolina, where he had numerous business interests including coownership of the local Holiday Inn. His future reputation among tourists was not going to be in the accommodations field, though. In 1960, he bought some property atop a mountain in Maggie Valley, North Carolina, with the intent of installing a chairlift to the summit. A family vacation shortly thereafter changed his outlook, however.

Coburn and his family made a trip to the West Coast, with Disneyland and Knott's Berry Farm as their ultimate destinations. Overnighting in Oklahoma City, the Coburns stayed at a Holiday Inn that was next door to Frontier City, a theme park with an Old West motif. Suddenly, Coburn found himself with cactus juice in his blood. "I had always been a Western fan," he later said, "and I went to see that town, and they had shootouts and can-can dancers and real Indian dancers, and it was all so exciting that I said, 'I'm going to build something like this on top of that mountain.'"

After completing his trip, on which he also saw what was being done with the cowboy theme at the Knott's and Disney parks, Coburn did some inquiring and found that Frontier City had been designed by fifty-eight-year-old Russell Pearson, who had also been responsible for creating that bulwark of the Ozarks, Silver Dollar City, near Branson, Missouri. Coburn quickly enlisted Pearson's expertise, and the two became a team that even Jesse James could not have defeated.

One of the earliest brochures for Silver Springs' mammoth Six Gun Territory theme park.

KEN BRESLAUER COLLECTION

Pearson was well equipped for his late-in-life career of designing Western theme parks, as he was a product of that atmosphere. His family had lived in the Oklahoma Indian Territory since 1905, and Pearson had over the years accumulated an enviable collection of authentic Western memorabilia, including private diaries from the period and costumes and props used by performers such as Will Rogers, Annie Oakley, and Buffalo Bill Cody.

Coburn and Pearson's joint venture in North Carolina, Ghost Town in the Sky, opened in June 1961, and less than a year later they set their sights on Silver Springs and Ocala. Coincidentally, this was precisely the same time that ABC was in the process of buying Silver Springs from Ray and Davidson. The most discouraging word came from the Bartlett Deer Ranch, who felt the town warn't big enough fer the two of 'em, but the local bankers finally agreed that anything drawing more tourists to the area could do nothing but help everyone.

Ghost Town in the Sky had been limited in its scope by the area available on the mountaintop, but the new property in Florida was so vast, and so empty, that it was a blank slate for them to create anything their imagination could concoct. And what a town this twosome founded: Six Gun Territory.

Visitors' first experience at Six Gun was the railroad station, from which the locomotives regularly departed. During the trip to the town, the

DAVID COOK COLLECTION

Six Gun Territory designer Russell Pearson *(left)* **and Western town tycoon R. B. Coburn** *(right)* **pose together on the dusty street.**

The part of Six Gun Territory that was next to State Route 40 was dominated by this sign and massive concrete mountain.

trains passed dioramas depicting various Western scenes, and passengers could expect either outlaws or renegade Indians to stop and rob them. Somehow the engineer always managed to bring everyone through safe and sound, and the passengers would disembark at Six Gun Territory.

Of the many Western theme parks that thrived all over the United States during the late 1950s and 1960s, none was designed with more attention to detail than Six Gun. The town comprised some forty separate buildings,

NEAL FRISBIE COLLECTION

The courthouse was the centerpiece of the Six Gun town and housed the park's administrative offices.

Six Gun Territory often used pretty girls in its advertising, just like 90 percent of the other attractions in Florida!

ranging from simple to complex. The centerpiece was the courthouse, which also served as the attraction's administrative offices. Surrounding the court-house square was a scene best described by Six Gun's marketing department:

> The Territorial church, which has been turned over to the Marion County Min-isterial Association for Sunday afternoon non-denominational services—the little red schoolhouse—the Palace Saloon and Theatre, complete with red velvet-covered walls, beautiful dancing can-can girls and the great brass chan-deliers—the Hat Shop, hats for every occasion—Morrison's Cafeteria for full course meals and snacks, or the Ice Cream Parlor and Sandwich Shop, for sandwiches—the old Frontier Hotel—the General Store where crackers and checkers will bring back old memories—the Mystery Shack, fun for all ages—the Marshal's Office and Jail—the old fashioned Barber Shop—the Archery Range where you can try your skill with a bow and arrow—the Shooting Gallery where you can test your marksmanship with a rifle or pistol—the Camera Shop, pictures and film for all your camera needs—the Gift Shop, gifts of all kinds—the Coffee and Do-Nut Shop—the old Frontier Gazette newspaper, where you can read your name in the headlines—the Western Clothing Store and Gun Shop—the old Candy Kitchen, food for your sweet tooth—the Territorial Bank, which is held up many times throughout the day by the gunfighters of Six Gun—the Red Dog Saloon where old-time movies are shown throughout the day—the Blacksmith Shop and OK Corral, where you may ride horses or the old stagecoach into the Painted Desert—the Wells Fargo office, where you may see a trail-worn Pony Express rider gallop up to

Six Gun Territory featured stagecoach rides, although not always with such a colorful selection of passengers.

the station, grab saddlebags filled with mail, leap to the back of a fresh horse and ride off into the distance — the old Fort, with guard watchtowers at each corner and sharp pointed logs to guard against the Indians — the Indian Trading Post and the Indian Village, where championship Indian dancers from Oklahoma will present eight different war dances throughout the day and evening — the Mexican Border Town which includes a Mexican Casino, a Mexican home, an open Mexican market, and the Mexican cantina where a beautiful señorita sings her love songs.

When a representative of the Florida Citrus Commission visited Six Gun Territory, he seemed bent on proving that Florida orange juice could make friends even of natural enemies.

No Western theme park would have been complete without periodic gunfights in the street, and Six Gun Territory shot it up with all the rest of them.

Boy howdy, with all of that going on, what else could anyone want to see? The gunfighters' routines were carefully rehearsed and staged, and several times a day the ornery owlhoots would rob the bank or one of the other businesses, leading to a shootout in the street with the marshal and his deputies. The trusty crowd-pleasing finish consisted of a skulking bad guy being shot off the roof of a building and thudding to the street below. It took considerable practice for Six Gun's stuntmen to learn how to perform such tricks without injury, since there was no cushioning to make their landings any easier. The streets of Six Gun Territory, incidentally, were surfaced with white gravel similar to that used by landscapers in flower beds, so the falling gunfighters' landings could be a bit rocky if not performed correctly.

Reportedly, it was the staged gunfights that caused one of the few bits of friction between Russell Pearson and the rest of Six Gun's administration. With his passion for Western authenticity, Pearson preferred that the gunfights be presented as realistically as possible, while almost everyone else wanted to play up their comedy potential to offset their grim subject matter. (Some adults today remember visiting Six Gun Territory when they were too young to understand the joke, and all they can recall is seeing people getting killed

Russell Pearson's drive to keep Six Gun Territory as historically accurate as possible must have taken the wrong fork in the road by the time these publicity shots were made.

in the streets while their parents laughed. Apparently the furor that rages over the violent video games of today had its counterpart forty years ago.)

The compromise between drama and comedy—at least while Pearson was still alive—was the character of Digger the undertaker, who showed up at the end of each skit to claim his prizes. According to the law as interpreted by Six Gun, the town undertaker was the recipient of any valuables on his clients' bodies, so some slapstick routines ensued when Digger would attempt to forcibly remove the villains' fancy boots and other accoutrements. There would also be gags in which Digger would try to cross the dead guy's arms properly, only to have them spring back into all sorts of unwanted positions. Pearson tolerated such shenanigans to a certain extent but would have much preferred more straight drama in the street scenes.

It is difficult to say just how much influence Pearson would have continued to have over such matters, because he died in 1964, just a year after Six

Each gunfight ended with the comical Digger the undertaker attempting to retrieve valuables from the outlaws' corpses.

Six Gun Territory moved a bit farther away from authenticity when it added this skyride in 1964.

The original Six Gun brochure had to be slightly modified to include the new skyride, which did look slightly out of character for the Wild West.

Gun's opening. Before he rode off into that final sunset, however, he designed one more Western park for his colleague, Coburn. That park eventually opened in 1965 as Frontier Land in Cherokee, North Carolina. Coburn continued to preside over his Western empires with the able-bodied assistance of his general manager, Page Robinson.

One feature that debuted at Six Gun Territory in 1964, and was replicated for Frontier Land, probably would have been hard for a purist such as Pearson to accept. This was a gondola skyride, of the type that was sweeping the amusement industry at the time. Now visitors to Six Gun could have their choice of the traditional train ride or the airborne buckets, which did not have quite the same feel of authenticity.

During the 1960s, Six Gun attracted even larger crowds than normal on days when notable

DAVID COOK COLLECTION

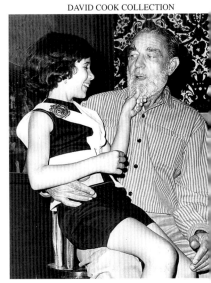

In the early 1960s, Six Gun Territory played host to numerous TV celebrities, including Buddy Ebsen of *The Beverly Hillbillies* and Frank McGrath of *Wagon Train*.

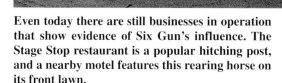

Even today there are still businesses in operation that show evidence of Six Gun's influence. The Stage Stop restaurant is a popular hitching post, and a nearby motel features this rearing horse on its front lawn.

television and motion-picture celebrities made personal appearances. No one was keeping an official list, but surviving materials show that among Six Gun's distinguished guests were Buddy Ebsen and Irene Ryan of *The Beverly Hillbillies,* Frank McGrath of *Wagon Train,* and—the biggest draw of all—Dan Blocker of *Bonanza.* Even Spider-Man made a highly unlikely appearance at Six Gun, capturing the bank robbers by throwing his web over them. No matter who the guests were, the crowds were always there to meet them.

Like Silver Springs, Six Gun Territory inspired its own set of peripheral businesses that attempted to ride on its coattails. Motels and restaurants in the immediate vicinity began playing up Western motifs in order to tie in, including the Stage Stop motel and restaurant, which occupied the property formerly traversed by the U-Drive-It Railroad. A few relics of this era still exist along Highway 40, even after Six Gun Territory long ago became a real ghost town. This process was the result of several factors.

SIX GUN TERRITORY

A COMPLETE WESTERN TOWN
A DAY OF FAMILY FUN

ALL RIDES AND SHOWS

FOR ONE ADMISSION PRICE

This brochure from the National Service Industries' ownership of Six Gun Territory reflects leaner times than did the lavish ones produced earlier.

Things were changing in the tourist industry by the end of the 1960s, and corporate ownership of amusement parks was becoming more and more common. In 1970, Coburn was approached by National Service Industries (NSI), who made him a stock exchange offer for his three Western parks. The deal was one he could not afford to turn down, so he sold Six Gun Territory, Ghost Town in the Sky, and Frontier Land to NSI and retired to Palm Beach, Florida. For the next several years, NSI retained Page Robinson as manager of the Western parks, who watched their declining popularity with some alarm.

NSI thought it had a good thing going with its three southern cow towns, so in the early 1970s, it began buying up other existing amusement

After Six Gun Territory closed in 1984, its contents were auctioned off and ended up all over Ocala. This former skyride gondola sits forlornly in a backyard.

Top: **This was the sad state of Six Gun Territory in 1986, just before the remaining buildings were burned down.** *Bottom:* **Believe it or not, this vast empty space is the former site of the courthouse and the surrounding Six Gun town, as seen in December 2004.**

parks and grafting the Western theme onto them. Two Pennsylvania parks acquired for this purpose were Willow Grove Park, whose name was changed to Six Gun Territory, and Rocky Glen Park, near Scranton, which became Ghost Town in the Glen. Do you see a pattern beginning to develop here?

Robinson could see that NSI was stretching the Western theme a bit too far, especially since by that point, the popularity of TV Westerns had hit an all-time low. When the venerable *Gunsmoke* last aired in 1975, it looked like the end of the trail for that genre.

In September 1978, NSI announced that its Six Gun Territory at Silver Springs was up for sale. The next few years were rough ones, and the cowboys and Indians finally packed up their bullets and bows in early 1984. (By that time, NSI had disposed of its other Western parks as well; Coburn bought back Ghost Town in the Sky at Maggie Valley in the late 1980s and continued operating it until 2002, when it too was closed down.) An auction was held to dispose of all the remaining vestiges of the Silver Springs Six Gun, and pieces of its dismembered corpse wound up in many Ocala area homes.

Six Gun Territory had existed in two separate parts: the section near Highway 40, where the train depot and skyride station were situated, and the town itself, which sat some distance back in the forest. The Highway 40 part of Six Gun was the first to go, its size and location making it the perfect spot for a shopping center. In the beginning, this complex attempted to retain a small part of its past by calling itself Six Gun Plaza. One of the largest collections of Six Gun artifacts had been assembled by Herbert "Boots" Hooker, the attraction's former barber. He continued to operate his barber shop in the new shopping center, using it as an unofficial museum of Six Gun's past.

In the late 1990s, to make it sound more upscale, the shopping center's name was changed to the Shoppes at Silver Springs, but at last report it had reverted to Six Gun Plaza, and plans were even afoot to give the complex an overhaul by placing false Western building fronts on all the businesses. Time will tell whether Six Gun can make a comeback in this fashion.

As for the town portion, after sitting abandoned for a few years and being allowed to decay, the former territorial capital was attacked by something even worse than outlaws and renegade Indians: bulldozers. But like John Wayne, Six Gun proved to be too tough for such antics, as the bulldozers were unable to push down the town's solidly built structures. In desperation, the entire complex was set on fire and allowed to burn to ashes.

Today the property again sits much as it did in 1962, a vast empty space awaiting new development. The only evidence of Coburn's beloved community can be found in the plowed-up sandy soil, which still contains thousands of pieces of the white gravel that paved Six Gun's streets. Occasional giant chunks of concrete that served as the footings for the skyride can also be seen protruding from the ground. Everything else has vanished as if it never existed.

CHAPTER THREE

Wakulla Springs
Tarzan Meets the Creature

It might seem that once Ray and Davidson proved that their concept for Silver Springs had real sticking power, other entrepreneurs would have immediately jumped onto the glass bottom bandwagon. But even though Florida was covered with beautiful springs, for several years no one came forward to develop any of them for commercial use to the same extent as Silver Springs. When tourism finally did arrive at the next one, it was far, far away from Ocala, and its approach differed greatly—although its influence definitely was felt in other, more familiar locales.

The story of Wakulla Springs is primarily one of how this attraction developed concepts that would be put to more famous use elsewhere. That, however, was not the idea at the beginning. In fact, when early settlers first became aware of Wakulla Springs, there was no such thing as Florida tourism—nor was there yet a state of Florida.

Although Wakulla Springs benefited from its proximity to the Florida state capital, it was in a rather remote location.

SEE *Beautiful*
Wakulla Springs
near
TALLAHASSEE, FLORIDA

NEW *Paved Highway*
FROM TALLAHASSEE
TO THE SPRINGS

This early brochure acknowledges that the lack of good roads was one factor hindering Wakulla Springs' commercial potential.

Wakulla might never have been noticed at all except for its proximity to the territorial capital at Tallahassee. This still isn't saying much, because to this day Tallahassee is far removed from the frantic tourist industry that drives the rest of the state. The reason for the seemingly remote location of the government center dates back to Florida's territorial days of the 1820s. At that time, the area had two major cities: St. Augustine, on the Atlantic coast, and Pensacola, on the Gulf of Mexico. The vast peninsula south of those two towns was a subtropical jungle that no one had any intention of visiting. Therefore, it made sense to place the capital halfway between the only two cities that mattered. It can reasonably be assumed that Wakulla Springs, less than twenty miles from the new capital, was probably among the first of all the state's springs to be discovered by modern-day Floridians rather than Native Americans or early explorers.

There were some early sporadic attempts to develop some sort of public facilities at Wakulla, but its story as an attraction begins in 1934, when the property was purchased by an individual who had no trouble affording it, even in those dark days of the Great Depression. Wakulla's new owner was Edward Ball, brother-in-law of chemical tycoon Alfred DuPont. Ball had been sent to Florida to make wise business investments for his wealthy relative, and he didn't do too badly for himself either. At one time or another, the Florida East Coast Railroad, the Florida National Bank, and the St. Joe Paper Company were all owned by Edward Ball.

Wakulla emulated its cousin Silver Springs with its own fleet of glass bottom boats.

WAKULLA SPRINGS COLLECTION

These fashionably dressed tourists somehow seem out of place on Wakulla Springs' jungle cruise ride.

Somewhat surprisingly, Ball did not pattern his Wakulla Springs development after Silver Springs as much as one might expect. The only real resemblance to what was going on down in Ocala was a fleet of glass bottom boats and a jungle cruise boat ride in the tried-and-tested Colonel Tooey style.

The most heavily promoted feature of Wakulla's jungle cruise was Henry, the Pole-Vaulting Fish. A promotional blurb from the 1940s gave prospective visitors a glimpse of Henry's act:

> Henry is the only real trained fish in the world, a big black bass. Forty feet under the surface is a cypress pole. Henry has his home right near that pole, and upon invitation—not command, for he is the aristocrat of the spring—he takes his short "run" and vaults over the pole. For unbelievers he does it again and again—the only pole-vaulting fish in the world.

Wakulla Springs Lodge, Fifteen Miles South of Tallahassee, Wakulla Springs, Florida

"Henry," the Pole Vaulting Fish—A Veteran Performer for Sight-Seers and World Famous for his Capers

Henry, the Pole-Vaulting Fish, entertained Wakulla visitors for many years.

This view of the interior of the Wakulla Springs Lodge amply demonstrates that it was meant to appeal to the upper end of the tourist spectrum.

Befitting his privileged status, Ball seemed bent on making his resort considerably more exclusive, rather than trying to pull in as many tourists as possible. A good example of this different way of thinking is the Spanish-style lodge Ball began constructing next to the spring in 1935. Furnished in a lavish manner, and with original murals decorating even the exposed beamwork, the lodge contained only twenty-seven rooms, hardly throwing out the welcome mat to any Tom, Dick, or Henry — be they fish or otherwise. Even though a fire in 1943 required a new roof to be installed, the lodge continues to stand as the centerpiece of the park today and still exudes the aura of old money.

Wakulla Springs might have remained a retreat for the wealthy and become a mere footnote in Florida tourism history had it not been for a move made by Ed Ball in the late 1930s. Somehow he became aware of the activities of Newton Perry at Silver Springs and hired Perry to be the new manager at Wakulla. Born showman that he was, Perry seized the opportunity to bring publicity to Wakulla in ways the property had never seen before.

Wakulla Springs' pedal boats were fine for those with the necessary leg muscle power to drive them.

Much of this publicity was a direct legacy of the relationships Perry had established in the Hollywood movie community. Because of his involvement in the motion pictures that were filmed during his time at Silver Springs, when he moved north to Wakulla, he somehow persuaded the movie crews to follow him there. Having already established himself with the Grantland Rice *Sport-lights* series, Perry set about staging even more elaborate underwater stories at Wakulla. Among these was *What a Picnic!* in which several teenagers were seen driving their jalopy to—and *into*—Wakulla Springs for a submarine meal. Most of the stunts Perry later staged at Weeki Wachee Spring were in evidence

This interesting pair of shots shows Newt Perry setting up the scene for one of his underwater acts, and the subsequent pose as enacted by some of his local swimmers.

Camera crews prepare to shoot another scene for one of the Grantland Rice *Sportlights* **installments.**

in this early example, including having the youths eat, drink, and exhale "cigarette smoke" (actually milk) underwater.

It was during the production of these shorts that Perry began developing other ideas he would later implement at Weeki Wachee. He devised a series of hidden air hoses that enabled his performers to remain underwater for longer periods of time, and he also invented the lesser-known "air stations," which acted as compression chambers for swimmers needing a quick gulp. The air stations proved impractical for entertainment purposes, but Perry tinkered with and refined the air hose idea over the next decade.

Besides his short subject experiments, Perry also managed to lure the MGM Tarzan crew to Wakulla, after working with them on *Tarzan*

Newt Perry demonstrates his air stations at Wakulla Springs, the precursor to his breathing hoses later used at Weeki Wachee.

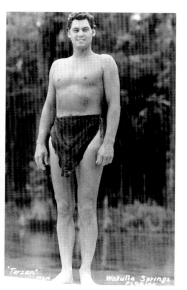

Johnny Weissmuller posed for this promotional shot while filming *Tarzan's Secret Treasure* (1941) at Wakulla Springs.

Finds a Son at Silver Springs. By that point, only two films remained to be filmed in the studio's six-volume Tarzan series, and jungle animals of every description were brought to Wakulla for the 1941 filming of *Tarzan's Secret Treasure.* Boys from the neighborhood, some of whom had probably appeared in Perry's short subjects, were pressed into service to appear as natives in the story. The second and final Tarzan

These Wakulla brochures illustrate the changing styles preferred by tourist attractions from the 1930s to the 1970s.

Wakulla Springs

LAND OF ROMANCE
AND MYSTERY

Wakulla Springs published this account of its history during World War II; it mentions that many female employees wore the insignias of their boyfriends' branches of the military.

epic to feature Wakulla footage was *Tarzan's New York Adventure* (1942), which largely took place far from the jungle. For the ape man's triumphant return home at the end of the story, Wakulla again stood in for Africa.

These films were fine escapist fare for a country that had just entered World War II, and Wakulla had its own part to play in that conflict. Unlike other attractions, which depended heavily on automobile traffic, Wakulla was not necessarily a "roadside attraction" in that sense, so it was able to weather the war years quite well with Edward Ball's money and occasional visitors from Camp Gordon Johnson, located in nearby Carrabelle.

Those soldiers costarred with the Wakulla scenery in one of Grantland Rice's wartime short subjects. In April 1943, the Camp Gordon Johnson recruits descended on Wakulla Springs to stage a mock battle that was intended to duplicate the conditions they would find when storming the beaches at Normandy. The sham battle shenanigans were filmed by Rice and released under the title

The Tarpon Club Girls from Florida State College for Women line up on Wakulla's entrance sign.

The Tarpon Girls put on amazing demonstrations of synchronized swimming at Wakulla Springs.

Amphibious Warfare, which won an Academy Award in 1944. Unlike most of Newt Perry's productions for the Rice newsreels, this one was not intended to be humorous.

While the war was raging, the soldiers were more in need than ever of having pretty girls to boost morale and remind them of why they were fighting. It was Wakulla's—and the soldiers'—good fortune that around the same time the war started, the springs became a practice ground for members of the synchronized swimming team from Tallahassee's Florida State College for Women. The team had been established in 1937 as the Tarpon Club, and its members were known alternately as the Tarpon Club Girls or the Tarpon Girls. Under either name, they dived into Wakulla Springs to practice their elaborate routines and were a sight for sore eyes for the visiting servicemen, whose eyes were certainly sore enough from the sights they had seen.

Though Newt Perry probably had no direct connection with the Tarpon Girls' swimming routines, it does seem likely that he picked up an idea or two that he could use once the war was over and he got the chance to start his own attraction at Weeki Wachee. At least, the concept of having beautiful females performing graceful routines in the water seems to have stayed with him. The Tarpon Girls' home college eventually went coed in the late 1940s and changed its name to Florida State University, which it remains today. The Tarpon Club

Who could resist a Wakulla Springs bumper sign when offered by the Tarpon Club cuties?

WAKULLA SPRINGS COLLECTION

officially disbanded in 1995, but it was revived after a fashion in 2003.

Once Normandy had been invaded as successfully as its stand-in at Wakulla and the war ended, Newt Perry moved on to his career-topping project at Weeki Wachee, and Wakulla was again left to fend for itself. While the rest of Florida was experiencing its unprecedented tourist boom of the 1950s, Edward Ball was mostly content to sit back and let Wakulla be an island of calm.

Breaking up the monotony of this era in Wakulla's history was the return of the Hollywood movie crews, but for a much different purpose than the Tarzan films. In 1953, representatives from Universal Studios, long known for their monster movies, arrived at Wakulla to scout out jungle settings for their newest fright flick, which involved a half-man, half-fish monstrosity inhabiting a remote corner of the Amazon: the Creature from the Black Lagoon. Young Wakulla employee Ricou Browning was asked to conduct the Universal globetrotters on their tour of the springs. Browning had worked at Wakulla earlier, while a teenager, and had recently returned after a stint at Weeki Wachee. He did not know it at the time, but Browning was to become to Wakulla in the 1950s what Newt Perry had been in the 1940s.

To test how clearly the underwater scenes would photograph at Wakulla, the studio execs asked Browning to swim for some sample footage. Browning did so with an unusual stroke that involved reaching only one arm over his head. When the test footage was checked out by the suits back in California, they decided that not only would Wakulla be perfect for the underwater footage, but Browning should play the fish-faced freak himself.

In the final film, the Creature's domicile turned out to be a joint effort between California and Florida. The underwater scenes were filmed at

Wakulla, with Browning stuffed into a sponge rubber suit, which he describes as "like swimming in an overcoat." (Talk about Creature discomforts!) All of the scenes that took place above the water's surface were filmed on the Universal back lot, where taller actors donned the paraphernalia to interact with the rest of the cast. Universal had decided that Browning's relatively short stature would not project the proper menacing image when placed directly alongside everyone else.

Ricou Browning was not the only one featured in the Wakulla footage. The script called for the story's leading lady, played by Julia Adams, to have some underwater close encounters of the Creature kind, so a more skilled swimmer was needed to double for her. To the rescue came Ginger Stanley Hallowell, also a recent Weeki Wachee veteran, who was being employed by Silver Springs for various underwater publicity work. In the proper costuming, she made an effective double for Adams in the swimming scenes, although viewers who compared closely could see that Adams's physical build suddenly became considerably more athletic after she dove into the water. The second Creature feature reunited Browning and Hallowell at Silver Springs, and they remained a submerged comedy team in publicity campaigns for quite some time thereafter.

Ball might have considered using the Creature's reputation to help promote Wakulla Springs, but by the late 1950s, he seemed resigned to the fact that the attraction just did not have the location to put it in league with Silver Springs, Weeki Wachee, or the others. Just when it appeared as though things

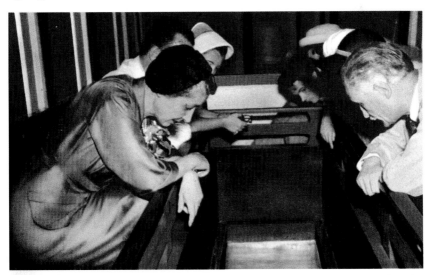

These tourists on one of Wakulla's glass bottom boats are probably expecting the Creature from the Black Lagoon to put in an appearance.

This 1951 postcard folder shows that things at Wakulla had changed very little since the 1930s.

Wakulla Springs might have been the most upscale of all the Florida springs attractions, but it too used bathing beauties to attract attention.

were never going to change, in August 1959 newspaper columnist Don Meik-lejohn gave his readers a scoop:

> Will the name of Wakulla Springs, a beautiful but relatively undeveloped tourist attraction 14 miles south of Tallahassee, be changed to Disneyland, Florida? Could be! There is a rumor that Edward Ball, trustee of the vast DuPont financial empire and owner of Wakulla Springs, has been dickering with Disney about such an enterprise. Disney was recently quoted as being definitely interested in Florida.

Meiklejohn went on to mention the recent purchase of Weeki Wachee by ABC-Paramount as evidence that large corporations were interested in Florida attractions, but as it turned out, Walt Disney was not interested in Florida— not then, anyway.

And so Wakulla retained its low-key character. Over the next few years, there were sporadic attempts to help shove Wakulla into the bright Florida sunshine being enjoyed by its spring-water siblings, but they all seemed to harp on the same subjects. In June 1962, the *Pensacola Journal* editorialized about a new highway that would provide easier access to Wakulla:

> By providing easy access to the springs, where facilities now are limited to a small lodge and gift shop other than the springs itself with its glass bottom boats and cruises, a tourist clientele can be built up which will rival the

Wakulla Springs Lodge, Fifteen Miles South of Tallahassee, Wakulla Springs, Florida

Looking toward Lodge from Bathhouse

Swimsuits abound in this view looking toward Wakulla's lodge from its bathhouse.

much-publicized Silver Springs. In fact, Wakulla Springs can do for Tallahassee what Silver Springs has done for Ocala. Anyone who has traveled to Silver Springs knows the numerous fine motels which have grown up along the highway leading to that attraction, and how much Ocala has profited from the tourist travel which has been drawn there.

Despite the Pensacola paper's enthusiasm, almost a year later the same song was still being sung. In March 1963, the *Tallahassee Democrat* bemoaned the fact that the state capital was being left out of the tourism boom that was making the rest of Florida explode: "Wakulla Springs and its jungle tour need yield to nothing in Florida as an exciting experience for a visitor, but it stays open more by a wealthy owner's sufferance than by paid attendance." The editor then went on to enumerate other Tallahassee-area attractions that faced similar problems, among them the city's Junior Museum and nearby Killearn Gardens State Park.

"The common lack is promotion," the editorial concluded. "They have to compete for tourist attention with the great publicity campaigns and billboard beckonings of Silver Springs, Marineland, Cypress Gardens and a hundred lesser attractions in Florida." Ironically, Marineland and Cypress Gardens both eventually closed due to a lack of tourist traffic, but that problem was nowhere in sight in 1963.

Wakulla Springs Lodge, Fifteen Miles South of Tallahassee, Wakulla Springs, Florida

Sight-Seers Paradise

Although this postcard promoted Wakulla as a "sightseers' paradise," the crowds never did reach the level of those at other attractions such as Silver Springs and Rainbow Springs.

The fake fuselage of a downed 747 jet was submerged in Wakulla Springs for a brief sequence in the disaster movie *Airport '77.*

While everyone else seemed to be looking for ways to bring more tourists to Wakulla Springs, the one person who did not seem to care one way or another was Edward Ball. In the late 1960s, he enraged a good number of locals by putting up a fence across the river four and a half miles south of the springs in an effort—apparently successful—to keep nonpaying hunters and fishermen off his land. Such actions only helped cement Ball's reputation as a curmudgeon, but by that point in his life, he could not have cared less.

Trespassers might not have been welcome at Wakulla, but the gates were still thrown wide open for any movie companies that wanted to venture that way. In 1965, Wakulla was used for scenes in the fantasy film *Around the World Under the Sea,* produced by the Ivan Tors Studio of Miami. Tors had already enjoyed an association with Silver Springs through his *Sea Hunt* television series, and by the decade's end, he would be comfortably ensconced at Homosassa Springs as well. Not coincidentally, the star of *Around the World* was ex–*Sea Hunt*er Lloyd Bridges.

Wakulla received even more publicity, but less exposure, as the setting for a sequence in *Airport '77,* one of a spate of big-budget, bigger-disaster films of the late 1970s. The phony hull of a 747 jet was constructed on the banks and allowed to sink in the drink to represent the downed aircraft of the plot. The entire sequence shot at Wakulla was to last four to six minutes, depending on which newspaper article one consulted. The movie's main star, Jack Lemmon, was on hand to appear in three seconds of footage as the rescue crew rallied to raise the doomed airliner.

Edward Ball died in 1981, leaving most of his vast holdings—including Wakulla Springs—to the Nemours Foundation, a charitable organization for children founded by brother-in-law DuPont. In 1986, the state of Florida

**When Wakulla Springs became a Florida state park in 1986, it basically contin-
ued what it had been doing for the past fifty years.**

expressed interest in purchasing Wakulla for use as a state park, and that feat
was accomplished with little or no fanfare.

Since Wakulla had never been a tourist trap, practically nothing had to be
done to bring it up to standards as a Florida state park. In fact, today the property looks much the same as it did in the 1930s, which is saying a lot. Even
Henry, the Pole-Vaulting Fish, still makes occasional appearances for the
skippers of the glass bottom boat fleet.

In a world of constant change, it's comforting to know that some things
stay the same.

CHAPTER FOUR

Rainbow Springs
Somewhere over the Highway

It is not surprising that other than Silver Springs, which had made its mark in Florida's sandy tourism soil prior to the Great Depression, and Wakulla Springs, the pet project of a millionaire, there was something of a lull in spring attraction development while the nation had more important things to worry about—such as having enough food to stay alive. Once prosperity began a cautious return, Florida's promoters were able to resume their customary ballyhoo.

Just a few miles west of Silver Springs, near Dunnellon, was a spot with the beautiful name of Blue Springs. Its conversion from a strictly local hangout into a famous tourist attraction occurred in gradual steps, and unlike the stories of Ray and Davidson and Ed Ball, no individuals stand out as being primarily responsible.

John D. and F. E. Hemphill were owners of what was called the Blue Springs Company at the time commercial development began to be considered. By 1934, some tourist attention had turned to Blue Springs, but the Depression nipped whatever budding interest had sprouted.

The story really gets started in 1937, when Ocala businessman Frank Greene teamed up with F. E. Hemphill to concentrate on turning Blue Springs into an attraction that could compete in the state's growing tourism tournament. One of Greene's first steps was to choose a new name for the development, as Blue Springs

What was originally known as Blue Springs was given the more colorful name of Rainbow Springs.

just did not seem to color anyone's perception of what the place should be. Instead, the new developers simply added red, orange, yellow, green, indigo, and violet to the existing blue and came up with the name Rainbow Springs. At the same time, the river emanating from the springs, known as Blue Run, was romantically renamed Rainbow River.

NO OTHER TRIP LIKE THIS ...IN ALL THE WORLD

Riding in complete comfort and safety five feet below the water's surface, a strange and wonderful marine world unfolds before your eyes while a colorful guide describes the everchanging scenes in his rhythmic chant. NEVER . . . EVER . . . ANYWHERE will you see such an amazing underwater panorama or enjoy a more thrilling experience!

SEE THE FASCINATING RIVER OF RAINBOWS

Rainbow Springs' underwater boats were its biggest attraction in the early days.

Passengers in the underwater boats viewed the submarine world through portholes.

The Hemphills had been running glass bottom boats over Blue Springs since the early 1930s, but Rainbow Springs made the first break from that tradition with a new invention known as the underwater boat. Whereas in the Silver Springs–style watercraft passengers had to look down through a window in order to see the submarine world, in Rainbow's new boats the tourists were seated several feet below the surface of the water and viewed the scenery through portholes. The boat captain, safely ensconced topside, narrated and described the scenes during the trip.

RAINBOW SPRINGS COLLECTION

Rainbow Springs officially opened as an attraction on May 14, 1937. Unfortunately, material from the park's first decade is spotty at best. A lodge building and tourist cabins, all built from the same natural stone material, had been constructed in time for the opening. The new underwater boats soon joined in the fun, along with the *Rainbow Queen,* a traditional glass bottom boat that carried passengers on a scenic journey down the Rainbow River. In later years, the

The underwater boats, combined with the natural beauty of the area, made Rainbow Springs one of the most restful attractions in Florida.

04 Scenic Falls,
nbow Springs, Fla.

This 1938 postcard promoted Rainbow Falls as if it were a natural feature, complete with Seminole women using it to wash clothes.

same name was given to a more elaborate rendition of the concept, an old-fashioned southern paddle-wheel riverboat that replaced the original Silver Springs–inspired craft.

Rainbow Springs was also quite proud of its waterfall, logically given the name Rainbow Falls. What is somewhat unusual from today's perspective is that early publicity made no secret of the fact that Rainbow Falls, "the only scenic waterfall in Florida," was entirely man-made. Rainbow Falls still cascades down the rocks today, circulating water imbibed from the spring.

As at most other tourist attractions, customers became few and far between during the lean World War II years. Rainbow Springs managed to hang on by catering to airmen from a glider squadron that was based out of the Dunnellon airport. Soldiers from Camp Blanding, near Gainesville, also made the trip to Rainbow Springs to take in the sights.

Once the war was over, Florida's tourist industry not only came back to life, but did so like an awakening giant. Most of the earliest memorabilia from Rainbow Springs' history dates from the immediate postwar years. One of the most important artifacts from this era is a 78-rpm record on which are preserved some of the spiels given by Rainbow's boatmen. These performances would have been lost to the ages had they not been recorded in this manner. The stated model for the speeches was the calypso style of the tropics, and it is quite amazing that the boatmen had to memorize such complex rhymes to perform for boatload after boatload of passengers.

On one side of the record is "Skipper" Manning Lockett, who piloted one of the underwater boats. His cadence is difficult to capture in print, but his speech ran something like this:

> Rainbow Springs is a dream land, it's a wonderland, it's a lost world underwater. Now folks, I don't know the language like you do, I've never been taught to orate, but Rainbow Springs is one of the prettiest spots you'll find in the whole forty-eight states. I've traveled all over the East, I've traveled all over the West; I've seen many beautiful countries, but I like Rainbow Springs

In this 1940s view, the underwater boats travel back and forth in front of the Rainbow Lodge.

the best. From Hawaii to Okinawa, I've seen many beautiful things, but I've never seen nothing nowhere yet to compare with the Rainbow Springs.

Meanwhile, above the water, Captain Dave Edwards of the *Rainbow Queen* was giving a similar routine to the tourists. Edwards's speech ended with a commercial for the rest of the attraction's wonders:

Now folks, when you step from this boat, we don't want you to think that's all. Just take a short walk, go down and see our lovely waterfall. Well, when you come to that fall the water will be leaping so high, it'll make you think it's rolling, jumping, jumping out of the natural sky. Then if you step from this boat and want to be filled with a thrill, just walk to the Rainbow Lodge that sits on top of the hill. Up there they're serving golden fried chicken and candied yams and specialize in Virginia baked ham. If you make up your mind and take time and dine, our lodge is recommended by Duncan Hines.

The *Rainbow Queen* began as a conventional glass bottom boat but later evolved into this nostalgic paddle wheeler.

Captain Dave Edwards's spiel reminded visitors to try the fried chicken, candied yams, and Virginia baked ham at the Rainbow Lodge. Yum, yum!

Rainbow Springs' brochures became steadily more colorful and artistic as the years passed.

This was most likely the last remaining Rainbow Springs barn from the period of Rock City ownership. It was photographed in 1998 on U.S. Route 41, south of Floral City.

RAINBOW SPRINGS COLLECTION

Is your mouth watering yet? The Rainbow Lodge not only afforded sumptuous southern cooking, but a view of the springs from its terrace that was billed as "a panorama unequalled south of the Smokies," in a rather odd juxtaposition of tourism imagery.

Or perhaps it was not so odd after all. At some point during the 1950s, Rainbow Springs was leased by one of the most famous attractions of the southern highlands, the venerable Rock City of Lookout Mountain. Just how this arrangement came about is unclear, but it most likely accounts for the otherwise tenuous connection between Florida and the Great Smoky Mountains.

As any southern tourism enthusiast knows, Rock City was famous for its black-and-white-painted barn roofs along highways encouraging drivers to "SEE ROCK CITY." A less documented fact from this period is that Rock City's leading barn painter, Clark Byers, and his assistants were sent down U.S. Route 41 into Florida to paint "SEE RAINBOW SPRINGS" on barns as well. These ads, however, did not catch on in the public's collective consciousness as had their Rock City kissin' cousins.

Rainbow Springs was fortunate to be located on a major north-south axis. In fact, U.S. 41 largely followed the route of the old Dixie Highway, the first highway established primarily to bring tourists from the Midwest into Florida. Unlike some of the other springs attractions, Rainbow Springs did not inspire any spin-off or peripheral attractions in its immediate vicinity; most of the business generated by Rainbow's popularity took the form of tourist courts, motels, service stations, and restaurants in Dunnellon.

Being tied so closely with the fortunes of U.S. 41 was a blessing for a good number of years, but it eventually became a curse—and Rainbow's ensuing owners, after Rock City had packed up and gone back to seeing seven states, probably had as much reason to curse as anyone. The fact that this was such a heavily traveled route meant that once President Eisenhower's interstate highway building program moved into full speed, old U.S. 41 was one of the first to be replaced by the new, streamlined mode of travel.

Construction of Interstate 75, which closely paralleled the Dixie Highway/U.S. 41 path from Michigan to Miami, reached the Georgia-Florida state

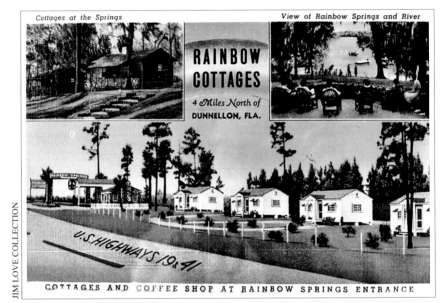

Cottages at the Springs

View of Rainbow Springs and River

RAINBOW COTTAGES

4 Miles North of
DUNNELLON, FLA.

COTTAGES AND COFFEE SHOP AT RAINBOW SPRINGS ENTRANCE

JIM LOVE COLLECTION

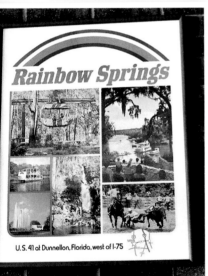

U.S. 41 at Dunnellon, Florida, west of I-75

Above: **The Rainbow Cottages were the most convenient place to stay if one planned on overnighting at Rainbow Springs.** *Left:* **Later, posters such as these were distributed to motel and restaurant lobbies throughout Florida.**

line in 1961. Each succeeding year saw I-75 being extended farther and farther south, siphoning ever more traffic off the older highways. All of the north-south routes in Florida felt the effect of I-75, but none more so than U.S. 41, which most closely traveled the same path.

Rainbow Springs began to see a gradual decline in its number of visitors, but at least for a while its sheer prominence in the state's tourism industry helped lure sufficient travelers the requisite eighteen miles off I-75. Other spots up and down Route 41 were not as fortunate. In 1967, the *St. Petersburg Times* decided to investigate how superhighway I-75 was affecting its neighbors, both near and not so near. The results showed that of the four major U.S. routes through Florida—19, 27, 441, and 41—the most drastic decrease in tourist traffic was felt by 41, with a drop of 76.8 percent between 1963 and 1966. It was also reported that in 1966, I-75 carried nearly three times more tourists than the other four highways put together.

All of these statistics translated into the fact that attractions not located at an interstate exit, as most were not, had to find other

ways to let whizzing travelers know of their presence. Weeki Wachee Spring, on U.S. 19, came up with a novel solution: In 1965, it incorporated as the city of Weeki Wachee, which gave it the right to have green directional signs at the proper exit off I-75. That gave other people similar ideas, and shortly thereafter someone started a campaign to officially change Dunnellon's name to Rainbow Springs, Florida. Tradition won out over possible economic benefit, and the name was not changed.

Even with the declining U.S. 41 traffic, in many ways Rainbow Springs experienced the height of its popularity in the late 1960s. As a matter of fact, former employees recalled that the attraction hit a plateau of sorts on Independence Day 1965, when combined ticket sales for the submarine boats and glass bottom cruiser ride topped $1,000.

RAINBOW SPRINGS
DUNNELLON, FLORIDA

FIRST, GO TO THE BOAT DOCKS and board one of the famous submarine boats (trips every 15 minutes) for the World's Most Unusual Boat Ride.

THROUGH INDIVIDUAL PORTHOLES you'll watch the unfolding of an underwater fairyland as the guide chants the story of this amazing wonder of Nature.

FISHY STARES will greet you as you ride dry and comfortable five feet below the surface of the water.

YOU WILL STEP INTO ANOTHER WORLD— mysterious and silent, inhabited by a myriad of strange and colorful marine life.

UNDERWATER FOLIAGE reflects sunlight in rainbow hues.

AMONG OTHER THINGS for the family to enjoy is the 5-mile cruise down Rainbow River in a glass-bottom boat.

ENCHANTING Jungle Trail winds around mossy oaks and tropical flowers bordering Rainbow Springs.

YOU'LL SEE the highest waterfall in Florida—another perfect picture setting.

CRYSTAL WATERS of Rainbow Springs are 74° all year. Restaurant offers delicious food. Gift Shop features photo supplies as well as souvenir items.

YOU'LL COME BACK again to Florida's naturally beautiful attraction.

The interior of this brochure enumerated Rainbow Springs' wonders in comic strip form, not forgetting to point out its location on U.S. 41.

What is this, Weeki Wainbow Spwings? This 1956 photo appears to have mixed the emblems of two unrelated attractions.

Rainbow's continued success in the face of the I-75 threat attracted some prominent, but rather unusual, investors. In January 1967, controlling interest in Rainbow Springs was purchased by Walter Bienecke, better known as the head stamper of S&H Green Stamps. (This has caused at least one wit to wonder whether the company's catalogs offered a vacation at Rainbow Springs for only five hundred books of Green Stamps.)

Under Bienecke's regime, Rainbow Springs embarked on an expansion program unlike anything it had ever seen before. One of the first, and most well remembered, additions was

A major addition to Rainbow Springs in the late 1960s was the Forest Flite monorail ride.

This magnificent fountain was installed at Rainbow Springs' entrance in the late 1960s, but today it serves as a planter.

the Forest Flite ride. This was best described as a monorail system, but one in which the passenger cars, shaped like gigantic tropical leaf formations, were suspended from the rail rather than riding on top of it. The Forest Flite monorail swooshed tourists around the perimeter of the entire park, most memorably passing through an enclosed aviary where dozens of species of tropical birds were housed. The waterfront, still home to the submarine boats and the *Rainbow Queen*, added more traffic in the form of simulated log rafts that were to give riders a supposedly rustic experience.

Rainbow Springs also gained a new entrance during this period of expansion. A fountain shot giant streams of water into the air against the backdrop of a multicolored rainbow; the sight was duplicated in at least one other fountain near the park's entrance building. A favorite prank for local high school students was to empty boxes of detergent or soap powder into the gushing fountain under cover of darkness. The resulting tide of suds that would cover U.S. 41 did not produce much cheer, but at least it kept the highway spic-and-span.

During the Bienecke years, Rainbow Springs joined Silver Springs and Wakulla Springs as a location of choice for an installment of the Tarzan movie series. *Tarzan, the Brown Prince* was partially filmed at Rainbow in the summer of 1971. The most memorable thing about this otherwise forgotten flick was a scene in which Steve Hawkes, as Tarzan, was to be burned at the stake. To produce more intense flames, the movie crew doused the wet leaves with gasoline. the resulting explosion was a bit more intense than they anticipated, and Hawkes ended up spending several months in the hospital instead of at Rainbow Springs.

Not all of Bienecke's intended improvements actually came to fruition. One feature that would have greatly resembled what Ross Allen had done at

Silver Springs was a proposed Seminole village. This would have been complemented by one of the most unusual features to be found at any commercial tourist attraction.

On January 7, 1966, Otis Shriver of Miami had somehow managed to exhume the remains of the legendary Seminole chief Osceola from his grave at Fort Moultrie, South Carolina. He then stored them until they could be returned to the Chief's home state of Florida. Rainbow Springs announced that its "authentic Seminole village" would be home to Osceola's new memorial tomb, and to that effect, the relics were placed in a vault in the Dunnellon State Bank on February 28, 1968, to await the memorial's completion.

The memorial concept was eventually forgotten, and when South Carolina learned of the grave robbery, the state pressured Shriver to return the chief's remains. So Osceola was taken back to his burial ground at Fort Moultrie, where he still rests in his eternal slumber today.

Undaunted by Osceola's forced retreat, Walter Bienecke and his staff soldiered onward with their other plans. It was announced that Rainbow Springs soon would become home to a model quarter horse farm, an outdoor amphitheater with a one-thousand-person capacity, and a two-hundred-room motor hotel. It was probably this last idea that got Bienecke a new partner, for around 1970, he sold 50 percent of the attraction to the Memphis-based Holiday Inn Corporation.

This seems like an unusual time for Holiday Inn to have been contemplating Dunnellon, since the motel monolith was busily engaged in putting up more and more rooms along the interstates rather than two-lane highways, but according to

This ad comes from the earliest part of the Green Stamps–Holiday Inn joint ownership of Rainbow Springs.

Rainbow Springs

It will restore your faith in Fairy Tales

Dunnellon, Florida

FLORIDA'S Rainbow Springs

Probably the final Rainbow Springs brochure, used during and after the opening of Walt Disney World in 1971.

veteran Rainbow Springs publicity man Joe Ryan, Holiday Inn was hoping to make a convention complex out of its new acquisition. Almost immediately after Holiday Inn got into the act, though, some unrelated events converged that would grind those plans to a halt.

When Walt Disney World opened just southwest of Orlando in October 1971, Rainbow Springs was probably the most immediately affected of any of its springy sisters. Much of this had to do with the continuing problem of its location. It had been difficult enough to pull people off I-75 and over to the spurting fountain entrance, but now that most of those interstate travelers were focused on Disney's wonderful world, with visions of Mickey Mouse in their eyes, no leaf-shaped monorail ride and bird aviary were going to distract them.

Disney was not the only culprit in this rapidly deteriorating scenario. Joe Ryan explains other factors that came into play at roughly the same time:

> In the Mideast, OPEC was raising its nasty head. In the autumn of 1973, I was at a meeting of the Florida tourism business at a hotel in Orlando the night Nixon went on the air and proclaimed that the oil crisis would dictate [a speed limit of] fifty-five miles an hour and limited gas sales, equaling gas lines for some months thereafter. That led the alarmed Holiday Inn management—who were already experiencing diminishing motel patronage wherever they were—to call a halt to expansion and to retract where possible.
>
> One such avenue was to tell Rainbow Springs to operate on a forty-hour week, thus being open five days and closing on Sunday and Monday. I was asked for an opinion, and I said that part-time closing in the every-day Florida attractions biz was like being partly pregnant—it wouldn't work.
>
> One of the business sources very big in Rainbow Springs' success was tour brokers, who ran buses full of tourists to Florida. One such steady source was Talmadge Tours in Philadelphia. They sent a bus to Rainbow Springs every Monday. I phoned Grace Talmadge with the sad news that Rainbow Springs would now be closed on Mondays, and her wonderful reply was "That's okay, Joe; with fifty-five miles an hour, we won't be there until Tuesday anyway!"

These three publicity photos, sent out by Rainbow Springs in 1972–73, give the impression that the park was desperately trying to attract attention in any way it could. If these couldn't save it, nothing could—and they didn't.

The corporate decision to close Rainbow Springs on Sundays and Mondays did nothing to improve the park's standing in the Florida Attractions Association, which strongly urged its member attractions to be open every day, helping promote the state's image as a year-round playground. Finally, in March 1974, Rainbow Springs was closed to the public, one of the first veteran Florida attractions to succumb to the new world order of tourism.

A little more than a year later, a reporter and a photographer from the *Ocala Star-Banner* gained access to the deserted park to see how things were faring. They found the paths being overgrown with weeds and the hull of the *Rainbow Queen* paddle wheeler tied to its dock. The birds that had inhabited the aviary had flown the coop, and the once-gushing fountains were so clogged with algae that even boxes of detergent could not have helped them. It appeared that Rainbow Springs was preparing to revert to the Florida wilderness from which it had come.

All was not lost, despite the grim outlook. The worst neglect occurred during the first decade after the March 1974 closure. Then in 1984, a company known as Chase Ventures purchased Rainbow Springs from the entity that was the latter-day incarnation of the old Green Stamps–Holiday Inn partnership. Chase Ventures seemed to have no definite plans for the property, but until something could be done, local garden club volunteers were allowed into the shabby and overgrown park to perform some maintenance. Incredibly, many of the flowering plants were still there, but so choked with weeds that even

Original *Rainbow Queen* Captain Dave Edwards was a featured speaker at the dedication of the new Rainbow Springs State Park in 1995.

RAINBOW SPRINGS COLLECTION

locating them was a chore in itself. The walkways were no way to walk either, and the rainbow-colored backdrops from the fountains had long since vanished.

After six years of work by the garden clubs, in October 1990, the state of Florida elected to purchase the Rainbow Springs property for development into a state park. The state acquired the fifty-five acres encompassing the commercial attraction, plus six hundred surrounding acres to serve as a buffer. The grand opening of the new Rainbow Springs State Park was held on March 9, 1995, with dignitaries representing all aspects of the property. An honored guest was original *Rainbow Queen* Captain Dave Edwards, who spoke about his long association with the attraction.

Today's Rainbow Springs State Park tries to walk a delicate balance between conserving nature and preserving what is left of Rainbow's commercial history. The Forest Flite monorail was sold around the time of the 1974 closing. The paddle-wheel riverboat eventually found a new home on the Ocklawaha River, and its subsequent fate is unknown. The state park salvaged some of the now empty cages where birds and other

Time has not been kind to the underwater boats, but work is ongoing to restore them as museum exhibits, if not operating watercraft.

wildlife had been displayed, and administration offices opened in the stone tourist cabins constructed in the late 1930s. The former fountain at the entrance became a planter, so detergent-wielding pranksters are no longer a concern.

And what about the famed submarine boats that were Rainbow Springs' primary distinguishing feature? Years of neglect reduced most of them to rusting hulks, but they were kept in storage as valuable artifacts. Incredible amounts of work have gone into restoring one of the boats to serve as a display; tourists will not be able to ride underwater in it, but they can peer through the windows from the outside and see a bit of what Florida tourism was like in its glory days. Seventy years after its official opening and thirty years after its ignominious closing, Rainbow Springs finally appears to have found its pot of gold.

CHAPTER FIVE

Weeki Wachee Spring
The Tail of the Mermaids

As it had during the Depression, tourism took a staggering sock in the jaw from that global conflict known as World War II. Established attractions were having a difficult enough time keeping their heads above the spring waters without worrying about any new developments coming along. Once the war was over and the soldiers and sailors began returning home, though, it was a different tale—and on Florida's western coastline, it was frequently a tail attached to the lower half of a beautiful girl.

That came later, though. Locals had known about Weekiwachee Spring for decades before it became a familiar name among tourists. Yes, in the beginning the name was spelled as a single word, and it was an Anglicized version of a local Native American term meaning "little spring," "winding waters," or "winding river," depending on which historical authorities are consulted.

Like many of the other Florida springs, Weekiwachee was a favorite local swimming hole and picnic ground, but little else. There is arcane evidence that during the 1930s, some enterprising souls had begun running glass bottom boats over the spring's surface, and reportedly a dance pavilion was constructed on its banks. But none of this had any bearing on what would eventually make the weird Weekiwachee name known nationwide.

Weekiwachee Spring apparently had glass bottom boat rides in the 1930s, but they had been discontinued and forgotten by the 1940s.

Champion swimmer Newton Perry, whose underwater escapades at Silver Springs and Wakulla Springs had made him a newsreel personality of some renown, had been glancing longingly at Weekiwachee since before the war. According to his daughter Delee, he felt that with his experience, he could build the spring into a tourist attraction from scratch. Perry had neither the financial resources nor the business acumen, however, and World War II forced him to put such dreams on hold.

As soon as the war was over, Perry joined forces with a business partner, Hall Smith, and the two of them set out to make Weekiwachee one of the first

postwar Florida attractions. After inquiring about, they learned that Weekiwachee was owned by the city of St. Petersburg and had been acquired as a potential future water supply. Since it did not appear that St. Pete was going to need the spring's water anytime soon, Smith and Perry arranged to lease the property.

During his time with Wakulla Springs, Perry's biggest stunts had been his staging of underwater performances strictly for the benefit of the news-

Newton Perry, formerly of Silver Springs and Wakulla Springs, was primarily responsible for turning Weekiwachee into a tourist attraction.

This plate must be one of the earliest Weeki-wachee souvenirs, as the name is spelled as a single word.

reel cameras. For his new Weeki-wachee venture, he had bigger plans. He was going to construct a complete theater six feet below the water's surface, and audiences could then watch performers enacting their routines through glass windows. It would be much like the view the underwater cameramen had experienced while filming the routines for newsreels, but on a much grander scale.

Residents of Weekiwachee's environs had mixed feelings about what Smith and Perry were doing to their beloved picnic and swimming spot. One of those locals was fifteen-year-old Mary Darlington, who was accustomed to coming down to the spring to swim. She was not totally unfamiliar with Newt Perry's name and reputation, as a "friend of a friend" in Tarpon Springs had worked with Perry at Wakulla, but she was not certain whether the rumors of him moving operations to Weekiwachee were true.

> I had heard that Newt Perry was coming down from Wakulla Springs to develop Weekiwachee, and sure enough, the next time we arrived to go swimming at the spring, it was roped off with Do Not Enter signs. Well, I was the first one to go under the ropes and search for this Mr. Perry who was causing all the trouble. It was no longer going to be the playground for people from Tarpon Springs and Brooksville.

Darlington canvassed all the workmen until she located Perry, who did not seem upset that his new property was being trespassed upon so quickly. Instead, he explained his underwater show idea to the group of teenagers and invited them all to return the following Saturday for tryouts to be in the cast. As it turned out, the audition consisted of nothing more than having the youngsters swim across the spring from one side to the other, something they had all been doing for years anyway. This swimming ability was the prerequisite to learning the stunts Perry would teach them later.

Darlington, her brother (billed as "Ed the Great"), her friends, and a similar youthful group from Brooksville were enlisted to perform at Weeki-wachee on weekends, inasmuch as they were still in high school and could

Ed Darlington, known as Ed the Great, and sister Mary performed as a team in the early Weekiwachee shows.

not be there during the week. To hold down the fort and be the star performers the rest of the time, Perry brought in two of his most trusted swimmers from Wakulla Springs, Nancy Tribble and Teresa Myers. Tourists who visited Weekiwachee's underwater theater on Monday through Friday saw what amounted to a two-person show.

Newt Perry's concept of a theater that seated the audience underwater was a novel one, and it made Weekiwachee Spring famous.

The early audiences for Weekiwachee's shows were quite small. Newt Perry narrated from over the audience members' shoulders.

Perry's new attraction formally opened in October 1947. Surviving photos from those early years show that the underwater theater concept still had some waterbugs to be worked out. Instead of the large, panoramic plate-glass windows that became familiar to later visitors, the original theater had windows that resembled a series of portholes. Audience members had to slide up to the very surface of the glass in order to peer into the watery landscape and watch the performances while Newt Perry stood behind them and narrated the proceedings in much the same way the newsreel announcers had done a decade earlier.

Such an arrangement would not have been practical had huge crowds been a factor, but in Weekiwachee's early days, the performers had a full house if twenty tourists were in the audience. On exceptionally busy days, double that many could view the show by having one row stand behind those sitting in the front row.

What really set the Weekiwachee performances apart from Perry's earlier work was his innovative use of strategically placed air hoses. By eliminating the necessity for the swimmers to have to return to the water's surface for a breath of fresh air, the shows were able to stretch the stars' time underwater to unheard-of lengths.

Eating and drinking underwater had been a Newt Perry trademark since his early short subjects for Grantland Rice.

This is one of the earliest known photographs of Weekiwachee's adagio routine.

The first Weekiwachee brochure made no mention of mermaids.

The show consisted mainly of routines already developed by Perry for his Grantland Rice films, only expanded to take advantage of the lack of time constraints. The swimmers demonstrated their ability to eat and drink underwater and enacted a number of graceful ballet moves that were enhanced by the buoyancy of the water. The adagio, in which one performer effortlessly lifted another above her head with one hand, appeared to be a feat of superhuman strength, but it actually was no trick at all when the weightless nature of both submerged performers was taken into consideration. It did make a fine finale to the show and gave the performers an opportunity to float back to the surface while holding the pose. Virtually every piece of advertising and souvenir from the attraction for the next sixty years featured the adagio in one form or another.

Somewhat oddly, in hindsight, one thing missing from the early Weekiwachee format was its later selling point as "Spring of the Mermaids." With both male and female swimmers in the cast at the time, seemingly no thought was given to the mermaid concept, which later became all pervasive. In fact, the earliest Weekiwachee

In its premermaid days, Weekiwachee's selling point was its "mountain underwater."

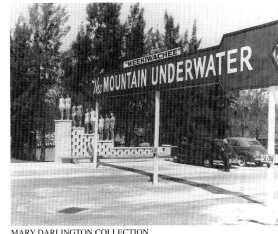

MARY DARLINGTON COLLECTION

DELEE PERRY COLLECTION

Newt Perry coaches Ann Blyth—minus her mermaid tail and blond wig—on the finer points of underwater performance.

advertisements emphasized its reputation as "The Mountain Underwater," a reference to the alien-looking landscape tourists viewed as the backdrop for the underwater antics. It took a singular event the year after Weekiwachee's opening to spawn the mermaid concept, which would come to serve it so well in the future.

Out in Hollywood, Universal Studios was planning a sophisticated fantasy titled *Mr. Peabody and the Mermaid,* in which a mild-mannered Bostonian (William Powell) accidentally hooks a mermaid (Ann Blyth) during a fishing trip near Miami and subsequently hides her in the fish pond at his mansion. His attempts to combat his friends' and family's natural supposition that he is either crazy or having an extramarital affair provided much of the comedy. Most likely through

DELEE PERRY COLLECTION

When *Mr. Peabody and the Mermaid* had its premiere in Tampa, Newt Perry took Weekiwachee mermaid Nancy Tribble along to promote both the movie and the attraction. This was the beginning of Weekiwachee's association with mermaids.

Newt Perry's many past connections in the movie industry, the decision was made to film all of the underwater sequences at Weekiwachee.

The usual Weekiwachee performance area seen from the underwater theater was used sparingly, standing in for mermaid Blyth's natural habitat in the open sea. Most of the underwater sequences supposedly took place in Peabody's fish pond, and for that, an elaborate set was constructed at the bottom of one of the other areas of the spring. These sequences were filmed by a camera submerged in a tank, while the others were filmed through the theater windows.

Perry coached Ann Blyth in the proper techniques of underwater breathing, and according to all reports, she was a quick study and a natural athlete. Though she performed the necessary underwater close-ups, her acrobatic swimming in most of the long shots was done by the Weekiwachee regulars, primarily Nancy Tribble.

The movie's release in 1948 was a big deal for publicity-conscious Perry. When the film opened in Tampa, Perry hauled a large water tank to the theater and had Nancy and other girls swim around inside. This not only promoted Weekiwachee's association with the movie, but also helped solidify the attraction's relationship with mermaids forever after.

Even as Weekiwachee was beginning to be known as the home of girls who were half fish, the cumbersome fish tails were used primarily for publicity photos. The underwater shows remained basically as they had always been, although the male performers were gradually scaled back over the next few years and eventually eliminated.

By the early 1950s, the attraction was beginning to settle into its future path. One of the biggest changes came when the name was split into two words around 1951. It should be obvious to even the most literate tourist that Weeki Wachee is easier to read than Weekiwachee, and this led to a change in its pronunciation as well. Articles from the park's opening in 1947 pointed out that the name was pronounced "Wicky-washee," but after the division of the word, most people said it phonetically.

It was around this same time that Newt Perry left his brainchild in the capable hands of others. His daugh-

The first version of Weekiwachee's entrance sign after the addition of the mermaid theme.

GINGER HALLOWELL COLLECTION

Weekiwachee Spring, Fla. On U.S.19 - Underwater View Of Mermaid Who Appeared In The Picture "Mr. Peabody and The Mermaid"

Nancy Tribble played on her stunt swimming for Ann Blyth in this promotional postcard.

ter reports that this developed from his publicity stunt promoting *Mr. Peabody and the Mermaid*. Perry was always looking for the next big thing, and the tank in which Nancy Tribble cavorted had given him a new idea.

Spring of the Mermaids

UNDERWATER SHOW!
60 MILES NORTH OF ST. PETERSBURG

He had an even larger tank constructed: twenty-two feet long, eight feet wide, and deep enough to install an entire underwater kitchen. Then he loaded this contraption onto a flatbed truck and took it on the road to state fairs, shopping center grand openings, and other such venues, basically re-creating his established underwater stunts for the masses. He billed his new traveling show as "Breakfast with the Neptunes," and even Perry's old employer Grantland Rice sent a letter congratulating him on his new venture.

"Breakfast with the Neptunes" eventually left the nomadic life and settled at Florida's Glenn Springs, where the audience was seated on one side of the springs and the giant tank was set up on the opposite bank so tourists could watch the performance. If Perry expected Glenn Springs to become his next Weeki Wachee, he was a melancholy mackerel when this idea sank. Perry next

Around 1951, Weekiwachee was split into the more easily read Weeki Wachee.

UNDERWATER BALLET

After leaving Weeki Wachee, Newt Perry helped develop a virtual clone of the attraction at San Marcos, Texas.

moved to the unlikely market of San Marcos, Texas, where he helped develop yet another underwater attraction known as Aquarena Springs. It would have looked very familiar to anyone from the Weeki Wachee neighborhood.

Finally getting out of the tourist business altogether, Perry continued his long tradition of teaching swimming classes in Ocala until he was debilitated by a stroke at age seventy in 1978. He died on November 22, 1987, and was recognized as the true Florida tourism pioneer he was.

Meanwhile, back at Weeki Wachee, things continued to develop and change. The biggest revisions in the way things had always been done occurred in the last few years of the 1950s. For the first decade or so of Weeki Wachee's existence, the performers had entered the spring simply by diving in from the banks opposite the underwater theater. In the late 1950s, a giant tube was installed that

No one should doubt that the Weeki Wachee mermaids were most athletic; the one on the left looks to have developed impressive biceps from her work.

In the late 1950s, a new, enlarged underwater theater was constructed to handle the ever-increasing crowds.

enabled the swimmers to gather in a small anteroom and travel through the enclosure until coming into the audience's view on cue.

Those audiences awaiting the swimmers' entrance had steadily grown larger and larger during the Florida tourism boom of the 1950s. By the end of the decade, even though the original 1947 theater had been modified to accommodate larger crowds, it was still deemed inadequate enough to require an entirely new structure. The new underwater theater seated more than three hundred tourists at a time, buried those spectators fourteen feet below the water's surface, reportedly cost $1 million to build, and had huge plate-glass windows that made it easy to view the performance from any seat.

What might have brought about some of these changes, or perhaps was caused by them, was that in 1959 the Weeki Wachee Spring attraction was purchased by ABC-Paramount, a formidable combination of the television network and the Paramount Theaters movie house chain. The Weeki Wachee brochures immediately began to feature testimonials from famous television and movie stars, and strangely enough, except for certain luminaries such as Bob Hope and Wernher Von Braun, all of the plugs came from actors who were currently featured on ABC-TV: James Garner as Maverick, Will Hutchins as Sugarfoot, and *Amateur Hour* host Ted Mack were three of the first to send their congratulations to their network's new baby.

With a brand new theater and ABC-Paramount pumping money into its new acquisition, the underwater shows took on a new, snazzy form that was far removed from Newt Perry's simple eating, drinking, and tightrope walking. Now featuring casts of thirty or more female athletes, the performances blossomed into lavish productions more akin to Broadway shows. This was quite natural, since Weeki Wachee had brought in choreographer Lauretta Jefferson, formerly with the Billy Rose Aquacade spectacle. Under Jefferson's direction,

Unbelievable Excitement and Thrills!

These were some of the slick brochures produced after ABC-Paramount purchased Weeki Wachee in 1959.

the Weeki Wachee presentations took on adaptations of famous stories such as *Alice in Wonderland* (retitled *Alice in Waterland*) and *The Wizard of Oz* (in which the Tin Woodman did not seem to be affected by being submerged). One trademark of these extravaganzas was the proliferation of elaborate props, usually made of fiberglass. After being retired, the colorful characters were placed on display in Weeki Wachee's outdoor Star Garden. A frequent performer in these shows, Bonnie Georgiadis, eventually succeed Jefferson in their creation.

With the increased number of cast members came another necessity: providing living quarters for them. Since most of the ladies had come far from their homes to perform at Weeki Wachee, the company felt obligated to make room and board a part of their job package. The Mermaid Village was set up in a remote section of the property, protecting the mermaids' virtue from those amorous males who might wish to follow Mr. Peabody's example and take one home with them. The mermaid living quarters functioned much as a sorority house, with strict den mothers to make sure none of their charges violated any rules of propriety.

Media types of all stripes were thoroughly confused when Warner Brothers' combination live action–animation feature *The Incredible Mr. Limpet* (1964) had its world premiere at Weeki Wachee. The story, in case you missed it, involved Don Knotts as a wimp who wishes

WEEKI
WACHEE

Presents

"ALICE
IN
WATER-
LAND"

The 1960s saw lavish underwater spectacles such as *Alice in Waterland* and *The Wizard of Oz.*

he could escape his humdrum life by becoming a fish. His wish is granted, and Knotts spends the rest of the story as a cartoon creation. Nothing about the movie involved Weeki Wachee in the least, yet a big event was made of its "underwater premiere," in which the film was actually projected through the windows of the Weeki Wachee theater. Knotts and numerous other celebrities were in attendance, and the event was captured in a short documentary titled

"Clamity Jane" was a retired Weeki Wachee prop who took up residence in the attraction's Star Garden. But no matter how much male visitors would have liked to take these specimens home with them, the mermaids were safely housed in their own living quarters in a remote part of the property.

Weekend at Weeki Wachee. In an unintentionally ironic moment, the opening shot of the documentary showed a car pulling into the parking lot—with a Homosassa Springs bumper sticker prominently displayed on the front!

Although the success of Silver Springs caused an entire tourism industry to spring up around its borders, none of the other Florida springs had the magnetic power to attract development of such magnitude, but Weeki Wachee came closest to hitting the tourists right in their bull's-eyes. Even before the acquisition by ABC-Paramount, Weeki Wachee had been adding other features that functioned in much the same way as Ross Allen's Reptile Institute and its companions at Silver Springs.

One of Weeki Wachee's add-ons resembled Allen's ventures in that it appealed to those who enjoyed creeping critters. The big difference is that the May Tropical Exhibit, alternately known as the May Museum of the Tropics, displayed not live, but dead examples of the strangest arthropods (in other words, ugly bugs) in the world. As if their mounted carcasses were not enough, the building was fronted by a gigantic Hercules beetle statue that was guaranteed to make the eyes of squeamish tourists bug out.

Another concept "borrowed" from Silver Springs was the *Congo Belle* Adventure Cruise down the Weeki Wachee River. The *Congo Belle* provided the best of both worlds by being a sidewheel riverboat with a glass bottom. Those who embarked on the cruise could see re-creations of life in the pre-tourism Florida wilderness, as well as short skits by performing animals. A similar idea, the Wilderness Chief Covered Wagon, was later added for land-lubbers. This was a barely disguised tram that traversed the backroads around the spring, stopping to let tourists interact with tame deer and visiting an "abandoned Seminole village," which at least saved Weeki Wachee the

The trademark adagio was re-created atop Weeki Wachee's entrance fountain.

expense of hiring live Seminoles to populate it. All of these attractions happily used the Weeki Wachee mermaids in their publicity, even though in real life those lovelies were never seen in their immediate vicinity.

Outside Weeki Wachee's property, development was on a somewhat modest scale. The Mermaid Motel opened across U.S. 19 from the entrance sometime during the 1950s; in spite of its novel decor with an ocean theme, a decade later it was replaced by a giant outpost of the Holiday Inn chain. Still doing whatever was necessary to tie in with the attraction, in some literature the motel was designated as Neptune's Holiday Inn.

BARBARA WYNNS COLLECTION

No one can say the attraction did not draw a wide variety of celebrities. Don Knotts visited Weeki Wachee for the premiere of his 1964 live action–animation movie, *The Incredible Mr. Limpet,* and Elvis Presley got up close and personal with one of the mermaids.

Weeki Wachee was a proud member of the Florida Attractions Association and had its own outstanding way of promoting that organization.

The giant Hercules beetle in front of the May Museum of the Tropics frightened both young and old.

The Wilderness Chief Covered Wagon trams took tourists on a jaunt along Weeki Wachee's backroads, stopping off for a visit at the "abandoned Seminole village."

Only a few other tourism entrepreneurs tried to muscle in on the Weeki Wachee mermaids' turf, but what they wrought sometimes became local landmarks. A man remembered today only as Mr. Herwede had a knack for building concrete dinosaurs and constructed a couple of them on Florida State Route 471 near Weeki Wachee. Actually, it was more accurately one and a half dinosaurs, as construction on one of the pair was halted by Herwede's

Holiday Inn opened a new location directly across U.S. 19 from Weeki Wachee and used many of the performers in its advertising.

unexpected death in 1967. The half dinosaur still exists as a silent memorial to its late creator.

Just south of Weeki Wachee, another roadside craftsman begat a giant pink brontosaurus in front of the Foxbower Wildlife Museum in 1961. The museum later became a taxidermy shop, and the connection between any of its incarnations and prehistoric beasts remained tenuous at best. Through several changes of ownership since then, the rose-colored sauropod continues to stand guard over U.S. 19 today.

Travelers in Weeki Wachee's bailiwick were out of luck if they didn't like refugees from Jurassic Park. Dwarfing the pink brontosaurus and his half-finished companion was a Sinclair service station built inside a giant concrete saurian. Sinclair had

This unfinished dinosaur was meant to be an attraction on State Route 471 near Weeki Wachee. The pink brontosaurus still stands alongside U.S. 19, even though its related attraction, the Foxbower Wildlife Museum, is long gone.

This dinosaur-shaped service station has been a landmark since the 1960s. The inset photo shows the building when it was originally a Sinclair outlet.

A Trip Through The

Old Lewis Plantation

BROOKSVILLE
FLORIDA

LEWIS PLANTATION
and TURPENTINE STILL
The Untouched South

by
PEARCE LEWIS

long used the image of a dinosaur as its corporate logo—in fact, it still does in states west of the Mississippi River—but whose concept the dino service station at Weeki Wachee may have been is a mystery that now belongs to the ages.

From today's perspective, what was the most puzzling attraction in Weeki Wachee's area actually predated Newt Perry's development of the spring by a decade or more. Tourism historians find it difficult to discuss the Lewis Plantation and Turpentine Still, on U.S. 41 just south of Brooksville, with any sort of objectivity because it so blatantly violates modern sensibilities. It began when local businessman Pearce Lewis was faced with declining demand for his turpentine spirits production in 1935 and decided to turn his homestead into an attraction for those who were traveling the famous Dixie Highway.

It is easy to tell why the Lewis Plantation and Turpentine Still did not make it as the times around it changed.

Paul Bolstein *(center)* **and his cast of Indians and gunslingers at Fort Dodge.**

Perhaps Lewis decided to take the name of the highway literally, because his new attraction turned out to be a re-creation of a southern plantation, complete with a large cast of African American performers. The idea of putting human beings on display is quite foreign today, but it was not so uncommon in the 1930s. The blacks at the Lewis Plantation were not really slaves—they only played them for the tourists—but the plantation fell victim to changing attitudes.

It is not surprising that it was a lost cause by 1961 or thereabouts, leaving the mermaids at Weeki Wachee as the only living, breathing (even if they depended on their air hoses to do so) humans on display in the area.

Other minor attractions were less controversial. Rogers' Christmas

PAUL BOLSTEIN COLLECTION

Fort Dodge was not going to be left out of the Florida pretty girl sweepstakes. This pair of Brooksville beauties promoted the Old Salty Mine.

Fort Dodge operated for only four years before I-75 took away its potential visitors.

House was unwrapped in 1972. Boyetts Grove was a local zoo with a wildly varied collection of wild animals. Then there was Fort Dodge. What? You don't remember Fort Dodge? Well, pardner, belly up to the bar and lissen ter this tall tale . . .

In 1962, about the time R. B. Coburn and his compadres were getting ready to shoot up the town at Six Gun Territory, just north of Weeki Wachee on U.S. 19 another hombre was trying to win the West in his own way. Paul Bolstein had worked at more different jobs than you could shake a six gun at, including writing comic book scripts in the early 1940s

Hi-yo, Seahorse, away! Who cared if there were no direct connection between pirates and seahorses when the buccaneers looked like this?

and owning a string of weekly newspapers in the years since. He also had a ranch and riding school at his home in St. Petersburg, which gave him the idea for his own Western park. (It is not clear whether he got wind of the impending debut of Six Gun Territory, which in any case was some fifty miles away and in no direct competition.)

Fort Dodge had much potential but never seemed to get past the infant stage. It had all the aspects so familiar to Western parks of the era, with a few novel twists thrown in to boot. Most popular of these was the Old Salty Mine, a three-hundred-foot stream that was salted with gold and silver nuggets and semiprecious stones. Visitors could pan for these valuables, then redeem their finds for cash at the main office. There was also Mystery Mountain, a cavern with scenes from the Old West depicted in fluorescent paint and illuminated by black light.

Bolstein and his family had big plans for Fort Dodge, but the opening of I-75 did him in. With no good way to pull people off the interstate and over to U.S. 19, he had no choice but to close down the attraction. This gave Bolstein a major financial burr under his saddle, but he hitched up his cowboy britches, took his gunfighters and Indian performers from Fort Dodge, and moseyed up to Panama City Beach, where he staged the same acts at that resort's Petticoat Junction for many more years. He eventually started two other Western parks: Old Bullochville at Warm Springs, Georgia, and Gold Nugget Junction at Lake of the Ozarks, Missouri.

Meanwhile, back at the spring, things were still going great guns, even if Fort Dodge had bitten the dust. ABC-Paramount must have been mighty pleased with the way the Weeki Wachee purchase had turned out, because in 1962 the entertainment behemoth bought Silver Springs as well. This opened up wide avenues of mutual promotion for both spring attractions.

Many souvenirs of this era were made in such a way that they could be sold at either park. Millions of kids fondly remember drinking their Florida orange juice from a plastic container shaped like the citrus fruit, and numerous examples of this ever popular item exist with a Silver Springs ad on one side and Weeki Wachee's on the other. ABC-Paramount was also the brain behind a publication called *Florida Pictorial*, which did not have as much to do with the entire state as the name implied. No indeed, all of the features in each publication revolved around either Weeki Wachee or Silver Springs.

Even ABC-Paramount's record label got into the joint act, producing a 45-rpm disc whose two sides were given equal importance; either side of the paper sleeve could have been considered the front. The two songs were performed by a group billed as Marlin and the Mermaids, and each took a different approach to its subject matter.

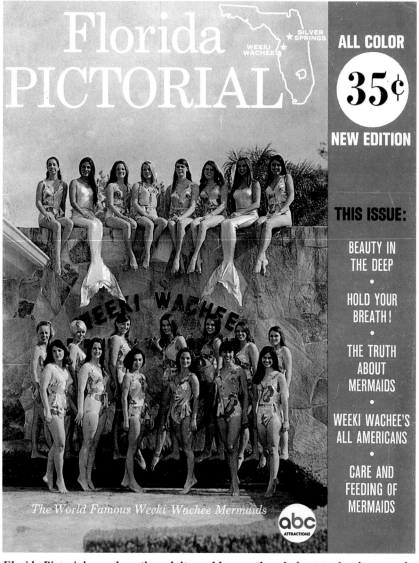

Florida Pictorial **sounds as though it would cover the whole state, but it was published by ABC-Paramount and featured stories only from Weeki Wachee and Silver Springs.**

"The Ballad of Silver Springs," composed by the famed Florida folk musician Will McLean, retold the Bernice Mayo–Claire Douglass–Aunt Silla version of the Bridal Chamber legend in verse. "At Weeki Wachee," by a songwriter credited only as H. Lyon, sounded much more like a commercial for the attraction:

WEEKI WACHEE COLLECTION

Alan Rock was the Bozo the Clown for Orlando. He taped segments of his show at Weeki Wachee, and they were subsequently syndicated to other Bozo programs across the country.

At Weeki Wachee if you think
    you see mermaids
Floating in the water so blue
Don't rub your eyes in surprise
    that you see mermaids
Because at Weeki Wachee you do.

Even the power of eight hundred-pound media gorillas such as ABC-Paramount could not stop the inevitable march of time. When the new I-75 was constructed down Florida's center, it had the effect of removing traffic from two of the state's most traditional north-south routes, U.S. Routes 41 and 19. Like Rainbow Springs on U.S. 41, Weeki Wachee also began to have problems.

U.S. 19 had been the main route from Tallahassee to Tampa, but now I-75 served that purpose. This meant that Weeki Wachee had to work harder to pull in tourists, only to see its attendance numbers drop in spite of the extra effort.

VICKI SMITH COLLECTION

Weeki Wachee entered the psychedelic era with this Day-Glo ad.

The adagio was still holding its own in the 1960s, even as the mermaids held on to each other.

Slowly the various extras the park had once contained were allowed to fade away. When a forest fire destroyed the "abandoned Seminole village," no attempt was made to rebuild it. The May Museum of the Tropics packed up its giant Hercules beetle and headed west to Colorado Springs, where the big bug continues to gross out tourists today.

The opening of Walt Disney World might not have had as much of a direct effect on Weeki Wachee as the I-75 situation, but it certainly was another factor. ABC had been the first network to lure Walt Disney into a weekly television series, and even more coincidentally, when the Disney studio began producing its own children's records in 1955, they were distributed by ABC-Paramount. Now the mouse that Walt built was making life difficult for his old benefactor, and in 1984 ABC sold both Silver Springs and Weeki Wachee to Florida Leisure Attractions. (In an odd twist of fate, if ABC had held on to its attractions for just a few more years, they would have become part of the Disney empire when the company bought the ABC network.)

Florida Leisure continued to operate both parks jointly until 1999. By then it had become obvious that though one of them held a silver lining, the other was a mermaid millstone. The company disposed of Weeki Wachee, which now had to survive on its own. But it appeared unable to walk as well as it could swim.

Things had really gotten depressing by 2003. The mermaid shows continued, but to an underwater theater that was lucky to be half full. The Southwest Florida Water Management District, legal owners of the spring itself—

Weeki Wachee celebrated the bicentennial in its own way with this 1976 brochure.

property ownership usually being different from tourist attraction ownership—finally decreed that the property was a health hazard and sweeping improvements needed to be made. That was going to be hard to do without income from tourists. The only part of Weeki Wachee that was attracting any sort of business was the Buccaneer Bay water park, which had been added during the ABC ownership; the water park sat over the spot where Ann Blyth's underwater castle had been in 1948.

Somewhat oddly, while its actual fortunes were in a tailspin, Weeki Wachee and its reputation began to be used in a generic fashion as visual shorthand for Florida tourism. A short-lived 1998 television series, *Maximum Bob*, featured an ex-mermaid performer as one of its characters. The title role was played by Beau Bridges, whose father, Lloyd, had floundered about both Silver Springs and Wakulla Springs in the 1960s. The theatrical feature *Sunshine State* (2002) also contained a bogus Weeki Wachee mermaid, who delivered the memorable motto "The important thing is to keep a smile on your face, even when you're drowning." More than one observer saw this line as an accurate assessment of Weeki Wachee itself, if not the whole history of Florida tourism.

In August 2003, the Weeki Wachee Springs Company donated the unwanted and unwashed attraction to the city of Weeki Wachee, population nine. The city, unencumbered by the need to use any minuscule profits to

As Weeki Wachee fell on hard times, elaborate souvenirs such as this plate were among the first luxuries to go.

VICKI SMITH COLLECTION

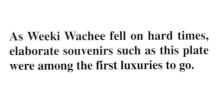

pay shareholders, began a campaign to preserve the attraction under the slogan "Save Our Tails."

As of this writing, it is unclear just what the future holds for Weeki Wachee. The mermaid shows, with a cast only slightly larger than the two-person routines Newt Perry began with, are still performed a few days a week. The Star Garden is gone, as are most of the other ancillary attractions, but there is always the hope that the booming market for tourism nostalgia will be the fuse that blasts the venerable park into its second golden age. All the residents of Weeki Wachee can do is hold their breath—but they have been doing that for almost sixty years now, so perhaps they will make it after all.

CHAPTER SIX

Homosassa Springs
Indian Princesses and Ivan Tors

The last of the "Big Five" Florida springs to become a major tourist destination had a somewhat uncertain start. In fact, it did not even receive its current name until some twenty years after its official opening.

Although the town of Homosassa had been founded in the 1830s, the local residents seemed to take the nearby springs somewhat for granted. This attitude continued for roughly the next century, with people using the springs for swimming and local leisure, but no attempt being made to promote the site to would-be tourists.

In the 1930s, Homosassa Springs was known as the local swimming hole and not much else.

WALK UNDER WATER!

NATURE'S GIANT FISH BOWL

A HUGE SPRING, 50 FEET DEEP AND [...] NG
6 MILLION GALLONS PER HOUR. THIS SPR[...] RMS
THE HOMOSASSA RIVER.
THOUSANDS OF SALT WATER FISH OF [...] ES
COME IN FROM THE GULF OF MEXICO AND M[...] IN
THE GREAT SPRING [...] BIG SNOOK, SEA TR[...] ER
JACK CREVALLE, SHEEPSHEAD, RED FISH AND MAN[...]

Walk under water at...

NATURE'S GIANT FISH BOWL
HOMOSASSA SPRINGS · FLORIDA

FOLLOW THE FISH TO NATURE'S GIANT FISH BOWL!

Trails lead through beautiful tropical jungle to the Fish Bowl, otter pool, ruins of old Yulee sugar mill and the various springs which form the storied Homosassa River, immortalized by the paintings of Winslow Homer. Picnic grounds, coffee shop and river cruises for enjoyment.

HOMOSASSA SPRINGS
Florida   On U. S. 19

Professional fisherman David Newell was responsible for opening a tourist attraction at Homosassa Springs.

The first person to see Homosassa's potential was David Newell, an avid fisherman who had won some renown for his radio program, *The Hunting and Fishing Club of the Air.* His angler's angle on the subject caused him to pay close attention to the springs, where a phenomenon existed that was most uncommon. At Homosassa, freshwater and saltwater fish could be seen intermingling, with no rational explanation as to how this could be.

Newell decided that this would be the big selling point for his new attraction, and after enlisting the help of some other interested sportsmen, he opened it to the public in 1940—not as Homosassa Springs, as one might expect, but

Instead of Homosassa Springs, David Newell called his attraction Nature's Giant Fish Bowl.

1—BRIDGE OVER FISH-BOWL

NATURE'S FISH-BOWL

NATURE'S FISH—BOWL, HOMOSASSA SPRINGS, FLORIDA

HOMOSASSA SPRINGS COLLECTION

The first underwater observatory did not have much room for people to peer at the fish and vice versa.

under the more unwieldy name of Nature's Giant Fish Bowl. The next year, he became editor-in-chief of the prestigious *Field and Stream* magazine, which certainly helped his reputation and that of his new tourist attraction.

One can almost see Newell's mind working as he searched for a way to make his Nature's Giant Fish Bowl stand out from the other springs that were experiencing such booming development at the time. Silver Springs and Wakulla Springs were seeing things clearly with their glass bottom boats, and Rainbow Springs had gone them one better with its submarine boats that put the passengers underwater. Newell got away from the boat concept completely and instead build an underwater walkway. Visitors were still submerged but could examine Homosassa's extraordinary variety of fishy friends through portholes as they strolled the walkway, rather than being at the mercy of a boat driver.

Nature's GIANT FISH BOWL

on U.S. 19
HOMOSASSA SPRINGS
FLORIDA

The history of what was happening at Homosassa—or Nature's Giant Fish Bowl— during the 1950s is quite murky, even if the water was not. Though it remained reasonably popular, it was certainly not a destination in the same class as the other springs. Running the

After Norris Development purchased Homosassa Springs in 1962, the company began letting everyone know of the sweeping improvements that were going to be made. The new entrance building and sign at Homosassa were finally built, complete with rotating fish.

spring was apparently more of a hobby than anything else for Newell, who continued to enjoy a career as a major outdoor sports writer for various publications up until his death in 1986 at age eighty-eight.

By that time, the park he had founded had long since gone through many changes. The story of Homosassa Springs as it became known to a couple of generations of vacationing families does not really begin until 1962, when the property was purchased by millionaire Chicago businessman Bruce Norris. It is still not clear just why Norris was so interested in the property or why he thought it would make a good invest-

HOMOSASSA SPRINGS COLLECTION

ment. What is certain is that once he had the attraction in his clutches, he set about bringing it in line with the other Florida springs that were doing such a big tourist business.

The first step in this process was to change the park's name to Homosassa Springs. Perhaps in a nod to the long-established appellation of Nature's Giant Fish Bowl, most of the ads for the "new" Homosassa Springs included the slogan "Nature's Own Attraction." Using this as the big selling point also meant that fewer expensive man-made additions would have to be constructed.

Since the area encompassed by Homosassa Springs was teeming with wildlife, it was not much of a stretch to incorporate this as one of the attraction's main features. Of particular stardom were the hundreds of squirrels that scampered about the property. Homosassa's literature made much of the fact that the squirrels were tame enough to take food from the tourists' hands. This was true enough, but what was intended to be the acorn from which future growth would occur started driving the park officials nuts instead.

One of Norris's first goals was to build a new underwater observatory.

At, "Nature's Own Attraction"

These wooded trails were part of Homosassa's new emphasis as "Nature's Own Attraction."

One of Homosassa's many Indian princess models tempts fate by feeding one of the spoiled tame squirrels.

HOMOSASSA SPRINGS COLLECTION

To make it more convenient to feed the squirrels, Homosassa installed coin-operated dispensers that provided handfuls of goodies for the bushy-tailed little rodents. Having virtually every tourist who came down the trail offer them a treat eventually affected the squirrels in the same way it would create a spoiled brat of the human variety: The squirrels became so accustomed to being fed that they turned aggressive toward anyone who did *not* offer them something. In other words, the squirrels went from cutely begging for food to demanding it. The little monsters would climb up people's pant legs and dive headfirst into purses and camera bags to retrieve the yummies they thought must surely be there.

The only way to remedy this problem was to remove the feeding dispensers and prohibit any deliberate human-squirrel interaction. The squirrels finally relearned how to survive on their own, but even though a couple of generations have passed since then, they are still relatively unfazed by all the activity around them and are quite content to play around people's feet when the notion strikes them.

Knowing that not every tourist could be dragged into the park by some nutty squirrels, Homosassa turned to that tried-and-true method of Florida promotion: pretty girls. All the other springs used this proven gimmick, and under Norris's ownership, Homosassa dove right into the cheesecake with the rest.

Looking for a different approach, but not *too* different, Homosassa decided that its attractive models would sport an Indian princess look. Established professionals such as Sheila Head, Karol Kelly, Suzanne Warner, and many others over the years donned the appropriate wigs, headdresses, and, most important, miniskirts that would have made any real-life Indian brave go on the warpath. This theme was also displayed on Homosassa's roadside billboards, one of which featured a rather novel idea: Tourists could remove the two-dimensional Indian princess cutout from the sign and put themselves in her place, standing

For a while, Homosassa Springs promoted its Crow's Nest restaurant with this attractive scourge of the Spanish Main.

on a platform and appearing to shoot an arrow at the Homosassa logo. (It is entirely possible, though this is only speculation, that the pose could have been inspired by one of Bruce Mozert's most famous underwater shots of Ginger Stanley Hallowell taking aim at a target at Silver Springs.)

Besides making the billboards more scenic, another accomplishment by Norris Development was a newer, more up-to-date version of David Newell's original underwater observatory idea. This floating observatory could accommodate more visitors at one time and had much larger windows to display the wondrous underwater world.

HOMOSASSA SPRINGS COLLECTION

At this "living billboard," tourists could pose in the place of the usual Indian princess cutout figure. For this shot, one of the models had the same idea.

Comparing this photo with the earlier ones, it is obvious that the new floating observatory had much more room.

While on vacation, have you ever stopped to write a letter or postcard to the folks back home, only to find yourself stumped as to what to tell them? Homosassa Springs did not want any of its visitors to find themselves in that predicament, so it came up with a unique solution: Preprinted "letters to home" were provided on decorated Homosassa stationery, apparently handwritten to give them a more personal touch. (So what if the recipient knew the sender's handwriting and realized it had never looked so good?) The letter managed to sound homey and friendly while playing up all of the attraction's main selling points. Let's open that envelope that just arrived in the mail from Aunt Myrt and see just what she has to say about her trip:

Homosassa Springs used this attractive brochure for its advertising throughout the 1960s.

HOMOSASSA SPRINGS

NATURE'S OWN ATTRACTION
U.S. 19 & 98   75 Mi. N. of Tampa-St. Petersburg, Fla.

E mbark on one of Florida's most unusual, natural recreational adventures . . . you'll remember your visit to Homosassa Springs always . . . and enjoy telling your friends about your experience.

Cruise the tropical jungle waterway . . . stroll along the unspoiled nature trail and marvel at nature's handiwork . . . feed the squirrels and deer . . . see hundreds of waterfowl . . . laugh at the playful otters and California sea lions (on a Florida vacation) . . . cringe as the 'gators and crocs leap for fish and marshmallows (yes, marshmallows!).

The excitement of the Gator Lagoon contrasts with the quiet enjoyment of the "Garden of the Springs" . . . here, you'll want to linger on the beautiful Homosassa River, among the flowers, shrubs and lovely orchids.

All This For
ONE SINGLE ADMISSION PRICE
Your Satisfaction Fully Guaranteed

RIVER BOAT LANDING WALK AMONG DEER GATOR LAGOON OTTER VILLAGE SEA LION SPRING

GARDEN OF THE SPRINGS UNDERWATER OBSERVATORY SCENIC BOAT TRIP TO SPRINGS WATERFOWL OF THE WORLD

ORCHID HOUSE

N

SEE IT ALL FOR ONE ADMISSION

HOMOSASSA SPRINGS NATURE'S OWN ATTRACTION

Commercial artist Val Valentine, already known for his work at Silver Springs, originally created this impressive Homosassa map for place mats in the restaurant; it ended up being used in every conceivable form.

Hello—This is really a great vacation and today we are visiting Homosassa Springs on Florida's West Coast. This area is so natural it is unbelievable!

The Spring of 10,000 Fish is the main attraction and this natural freshwater spring flows 6,000,000 gallons of water every hour to form the Homosassa River. It is the only known place in the world where literally thousands of freshwater and saltwater fish congregate all year, free to come and go into the river or the Gulf nine miles away. 34 different varieties have been identified here.

Comfortable pontoon deck boats took us down a beautiful winding waterway through a lush Florida forest. We stopped by Goat Island and watched as our captain released food from a high tower. We were able to photograph a 'barrel full of monkeys' at Monkey Landing as they ate peanuts tossed into a barrel for them.

One of the exciting things I've seen is the alligator feeding. These huge monsters jump out of the water to take their food and often munch a tiny marshmallow which is tossed into the water by visitors.

We saw waterfowl from all parts of the world, watched chimps at play, fed tame deer, goats, squirrels, barking sea lions, playful otters, and just had so much fun.

The flowers in the Garden of the Springs were beautiful and they have plants that bloom every month of the year.

You'll have to come see it, and the best part of it all, Homosassa Springs has something of interest for everyone, whether young or young at heart.

Sure hope everyone is fine there and we'll see you soon.

Best wishes,
[blank space]

Homosassa's pontoon boats took visitors on a romantic trip through the Florida forest. What, no glass bottom? The boats stopped at Monkey Landing so that the driver could feed peanuts to the little primates.

"My girlfriend was arrested for feeding the goats at Homosassa Springs."
"Why did they arrest her for that?"
"She was feeding them to the alligators."

Homosassa's entrance fountain was a thing of beauty after sunset.

All the other springs managed to attract moviemaking as a source of publicity, and Homosassa was not going to be left out of this lucrative industry. When it brought in a movie company, it might have unwittingly started a process that would dramatically change Florida's tourism industry.

When Disney camera crews first stormed the swamps around Homosassa to film scenes for episodes of the weekly *Wonderful World of Color* television series, Walt Disney Productions had not yet begun buying up thousands of acres of swampland near Orlando to turn them into a fantasy land—not to mention a frontier land, an adventure land, and a tomorrow land—but that's another story. "The Wahoo Bobcat" aired in October 1963, followed by "The Legend of El Blanco" in September 1966. The earlier of the two stories was filmed almost entirely in the Homosassa area, which was doubling as the Okefenokee Swamp. In the second, Homosassa

Tourists never tired of watching the alligators being fed at Homosassa.

The color looks almost artificial in this photo of a pontoon boat making its way through the Florida jungle.

HOMOSASSA SPRINGS COLLECTION

had to share screen time with Busch Gardens, Monkey Jungle, and the area around Brooksville. Is it possible that these productions were what drew Walt Disney's attention to central Florida in the first place? Probably not, but they certainly gave his company a chance to test the waters before moving ahead.

This taste of Hollywood apparently left Bruce Norris hungry for more, because his next business step brought about another major change in the way Homosassa marketed itself. Sometime around 1968, Norris bought the controlling amount of stock in Ivan Tors Productions, based out of Miami Beach.

Ivan Tors was very much a producer in the Walt Disney vein when it came to fantasy films. Born in Hungary in 1916, he had established himself first in the science fiction genre, with such out-of-this world features as *The Magnetic Monster* (1953) and *Gog* (1954), as well as his first TV series, *Science Fiction Theater* (1955). Tors was well familiar with Florida, having already placed Lloyd Bridges underwater at Silver Springs for the *Sea Hunt* television series.

In the mid-1960s, Tors began to diversify from the sci-fi realm into the animal world, initially with two theatrical features that later evolved into the TV series *Flipper*. The show about the popular porpoise who was probably smarter than his human costars was created in part by our old friend Ricou Browning, who seemingly had something to do at each of the Florida springs.

The success of *Flipper* flipped Ivan Tors Productions into animal films and TV series for the rest of the decade. Often the two would cross-pollinate, with the characters from one medium almost immediately turning up in the other. For example, the theatrical feature *Clarence, the Cross-Eyed Lion* (1965)

Model Marilyn Oliver cuddles up to Gentle Ben as if he were a teddy bear.

whelped the TV series *Daktari* (1966), and a feature film called *Gentle Giant* (1967), starring a bear in the title role, soon planted the plantigrade in his own series, *Gentle Ben,* later that same year. Tors had many other animal celebrities that, though not fortunate enough to have their own movies or series named after them, became an integral part of the 1960s entertainment scene in such productions as *Zebra in the Kitchen* (1965), *A Cowboy in Africa* (1967), and *Island of the Lost* (1967). At the time of the Norris-Tors partnership, the studio was finishing work on the comedy feature *Hello Down There* (1969), accurately described as "Flipper meets the Partridge Family," with Ricou Browning as second unit director for the underwater scenes.

HOMOSASSA SPRINGS COLLECTION

Clarence the Cross-Eyed Lion, star of his own movie and the *Daktari* TV series, was the mane attraction at Homosassa in the late 1960s. Costar Judy the Chimp played second banana.

And we all thought elephants preferred peanuts to cheesecake.

So now Bruce Norris had easy access to the Tors output and all of its component furry stars. How to make best use of this asset was the main question, although at least one article speculated that Homosassa Springs might become a theme park called Torsland. By this time, most of the series in which the beasts had starred had ceased production and were resting comfortably in reruns, while the animals cooled their paws by resting on their haunches. Clarence the lion, Gentle Ben the bear, Judy the chimp, Lucifer the hippopotamus, and numerous others were making a living for Tors by touring fairs and making other public appearances, and it now was decided that

HOMOSASSA SPRINGS COLLECTION

they would be housed at Homosassa between gigs. This gave Homosassa a new reputation as Ivan Tors's Animal Actors Training Studio, although in reality it was more of a retirement home for the hirsute thespians.

It was no one's fault that this new alignment between Tors and Homosassa came about at the same time that the combined one-two punch of the openings of I-75 and Walt Disney World was about to knock out some of the supports that gave Homosassa its toehold in the tourist world. Norris Development had done its part to help make the springs a vacation destination by opening a Sheraton hotel and the Riverside Villas motel nearby, but by 1978, the company could see that it was going nowhere fast with Homosassa.

Between 1978 and 1984, the attraction underwent several ownership changes that did not seem to greatly improve business, or hurt it, for that matter. Finally, in 1984, in a move that seemed to have worked well for other former springs attractions that were having trouble keeping their heads above the

This souvenir pennant comes from the days after Norris Development sold Homosassa Springs in 1978.

HOMOSASSA SPRINGS COLLECTION

In the years following the sellout by Norris, things got a bit shabby around Homosassa.

water, Citrus County purchased the property, soon changing its name (again) from Homosassa Springs to Nature World. The attraction began taking a more active role in the rescue, care, and breeding of the endangered, so-ugly-they're-cute manatees, with the ultimate goal appearing to be to have the park primed for takeover by the state.

The prospect of Homosassa becoming a state park elated some and worried others. By that point, most of the Tors animals either had reached old age and gone on to their final performances or else had been transferred to zoos where more professional care was assured. Lucifer the hippo still splashed contentedly in his Homosassa pool, though, and locals were afraid that should the park come under state control, the potbellied 'potamus would be shown the very wide gate.

All the details were finally worked out, and the state of Florida officially took over Homosassa Springs on New Year's Day 1989. Pains were taken to assure the public that the new Homosassa Springs State Wildlife Park was not going to make drastic changes in the way anything was done, except in those areas that needed improvement in the first place. The manatee program was to be enhanced to take advantage of this selling point, dilapidated cages would be repaired or replaced, and more native Florida animals would be brought in for the public to meet. And Lucifer the hippo would be allowed to remain in his

Even though all the other animal actors have long since departed, Lucifer the hippo, now in his late forties, continues to reside at Homosassa.

HOMOSASSA SPRINGS COLLECTION

Today's Homosassa Springs State Wildlife Park features a nostalgic re-creation of the original Indian princess billboard.

longtime home; at last report, the Tors studio veteran was still holding his own in his late forties, and if he missed the companionship of Clarence, Judy, Ben, and the others, he was keeping it to himself.

Today's Homosassa Springs looks much as it always did, except for the omission of certain problematic features such as the barrel of monkeys during the boat cruises. (The monkeys had become as spoiled by human interaction as the squirrels and had gone from primates to pests.) The entrance buildings constructed by Norris Development during the original big push in the early 1960s remain virtually unchanged, although the elaborate electric sign with its rotating fiberglass fish no longer beckons to passing motorists. (The fish reportedly rests in storage, awaiting some future use.) Even the old "living billboard" has been re-created next to the parking lot, giving a glimpse of the miniskirted Indian princess once more.

Tourists still flock to Homosassa to view the manatee program and other wildlife, say hello to the hippo, and walk underwater in the floating observatory. If David Newell and Bruce Norris were still around to see what has been done with their park, they would no doubt be pleased that the ideas they set in motion have continued to prove the timeless appeal of nature, even into the twenty-first century.

CHAPTER SEVEN

And a Host of Others

The Popular and Unpopular

When the landlady in Ocala told Rock City founder Garnet Carter that there was nothing particularly special about Silver Springs, as there were springs like that all over Florida, she might have been erroneous in her estimate of Silver Springs' future reputation, but she was absolutely correct in the rest of her observation. Silver Springs, Wakulla Springs, Rainbow Springs, Weeki Wachee Spring, and Homosassa Springs were considered Florida's "Big Five" and received the most publicity via radio, television, motion pictures, brochures, postcards, and souvenirs. Over the course of the last eighty years, however, numerous other springs tried for a slice of the tourism pie.

Sanlando Springs opened in 1925 but never became as much of a tourism legend as Florida's "Big Five" springs.

KEN BRESLAUER COLLECTION

Florida's Fairyland, Sanlando Springs, between Sanford and Orlando

Sanlando Springs was a beautiful spot but did not have much to offer in the way of commercial attractions.

Probably the first attraction to emerge after Ray and Davidson demonstrated just what they had in mind was Sanlando Springs, located at Longwood, halfway between Sanford and Orlando, hence the spliced name of Sanlando. The attraction opened around 1925 and boasted all the usual features of such parks—except, strangely, it did not have glass bottom boats, as one might assume. One of its early postcards gave its marketing pitch and enumerated some of its sights:

> Sanlando Springs has achieved its greatest fame from the unspoiled semi-tropic beauty of its 100 acres, augmented by rich displays of floral color, the fascinating paths through forest wild, along winding river, over rustic bridges, past lily-pools, through delightful gardens. In their season, azaleas, gardenias and all the rest offer their beauty and fragrance.

Such a low-key approach was practically asking for trouble when Mickey, Goofy, and the gang set up camp and castle only a few miles from Sanlando Springs, and sure enough, in 1972, the property was sold to a real estate developer. According to tourism historians, the only reminder of the attraction on its former property is a commercial development known as "The Springs."

An even more ignominious end awaited the tourist development around Fanning Springs, which had the good fortune to be situated where U.S. 19 crossed the Suwannee River. This was the home of the Suwannee River Jungle Drive, an attraction founded by Marx Chaney shortly after World War II. Like any good attraction, Fanning Springs had its own tourist cottages, restaurants, and gift shops, plus a boardwalk through the swamp and horse-drawn carriage rides through the surrounding forest.

This was one of the first places to be decimated by I-75's replacement of U.S. 19 as a major north-south tourist route. Even powerhouse attractions such as Homosassa Springs and Weeki Wachee had their problems, but Fanning Springs, with its lower profile, was hit particularly hard. In its 1967 report on how the interstates were changing the face of Florida tourism, the *St. Petersburg Times* had this depressing news about Fanning Springs:

> A once-busy tourist economy has just about disappeared. . . . Boats used to take visitors for rides up the river. There are no boats anymore. . . . A gift shop, then part of the Jungle Drive complex, is now a church. The drive is overgrown with high grass. The carriages stand rusting in an open-sided shed.

Below: **The Suwannee River Jungle Drive at Fanning Springs was a popular stopover for tourists on U.S. 19.**

The Atmosphere of the Beautiful River Immortalized by Stephen Foster, Seems to come to Life with a Visit to the

Suwannee River Jungle Drive

UPON starting this unforgetable three mile trip one is greeted by a genuine "old timey" colored driver in a high top hat, and assisted into a surrey with all the courtesy of the "real down South" of Foster's time. Midst moss hung Live Oaks and Cypress trees and song of birds, the drive is begun. It leads into a natural setting of scenic beauty and interest that could never be imagined or dreamed of by driving along a paved highway. Beautiful holly groves, yaupon, tupelo, magnolia, haw, gums — dozens of varieties of trees, shrubs, orchids and wild flowers are along the way.

Photo Courtesy Florida Advertising Commission

BRING A CAMERA

Surries with Drivers are available seven days a week from 7:00 A.M. to one half hour before sundown to transport you along the Jungle Drive beside the Suwannee River.
Also! Take a boat-ride Way Down Upon the Suwannee River!
Located U S Highway 19 near Old Town, 112 miles south of Tallahassee, Florida.

Florida Speaks "Foto-Fold"

Above: **The Jungle Drive brochure gives a sample of the features that were wiped out when I-75 replaced U.S. 19 as a major north-south Florida route.**

In 1950, White Springs became home to the Stephen Foster Memorial. The carillon tower was added thirteen years later.

As in other areas, the loss of the major tourist draw spelled doom for related businesses as well. The newspaper reported that in the immediate area of Fanning Springs, three service stations and a restaurant had closed, and the thirty-unit Suwannee Gables Motel and its connected restaurant were up for sale. Driving through Fanning Springs today, you would never guess that it once played host to carloads of happy travelers, as it looks much like any other small town along an obsolete U.S. highway.

All was not doom and gloom for the entire length of the Suwannee, though. At White Springs, on U.S. 41, the Stephen Foster Memorial was established in 1950 as a tribute to the songwriter who made the river's name a part of American pop culture—this despite the fact that historians are fairly positive that Foster never ventured anywhere near the area himself!

The Stephen Foster Memorial was a bit unusual in that it was a project of the state rather than a commercial developer, yet it provided more creative displays than one would expect from such a background. Among its highlights were a series of animated dioramas depicting scenes from Foster's

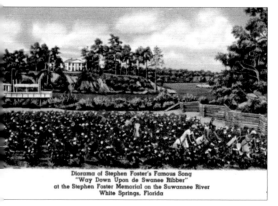

Diorama of Stephen Foster's Famous Song
"Way Down Upon de Swanee Ribber"
at the Stephen Foster Memorial on the Suwannee River
White Springs, Florida

The Stephen Foster Memorial contained these animated dioramas illustrating Foster's famous songs, such as "Old Folks at Home" and "Old Dog Tray."

Although operated by the state of Florida, the Stephen Foster Memorial played out its theme as well as any amusement park. Southern belles and paddle-wheel riverboats helped set the proper atmosphere.

songs, including "Old Dog Tray," "Open Thy Lattice Love," "Camptown Races" (doo-dah, doo-dah), and of course, "Old Folks at Home" (known by its opening line, "Way down upon de Swanee Ribber"). These scenes definitely predated Disney's Audio-Animatronic figures by at least a decade. A two hundred–foot carillon tower was added in 1963, and the park became the site of the annual Florida Folk Festival. Being a ward of the state probably helped the Stephen Foster Memorial weather the rough financial seas experienced by its less fortunate brethren, but the fact that U.S. 41 and I-75 run within less than five miles of each other at that point was undoubtedly a big help too.

It would appear that no amount of help could have saved a more-than-commercial attraction that opened at Sarasota in 1955. Now think

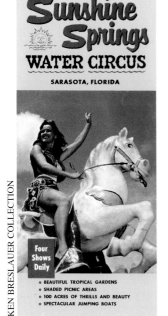

Welcome to Sunshine Springs, which has been called in print "one of the most spectacular failures in Florida tourism history."

These photos indicate why Sunshine Springs so strongly resembled Cypress Gardens on steroids.

about this for a moment: If you were an aspiring tourism promoter who wanted to come up with the most all-encompassing name possible for a Florida attraction, and you did not mind it sounding like dozens of other places, what would you call it? How about Floridaland? Well, that's a good one, but someone else came up with it. Here's a hint: Since Florida is known as the Sunshine State, and the biggest attractions of the day were the springs, why not call your park Sunshine Springs? Why not, indeed?

Sunshine Springs ignored one fact that set it apart from all the others: It was not a real spring! Instead, Boston developer Leonard Tanner bought a hundred acres of ranch land and set out to create his own springs attraction where one had not existed before. Sunshine Springs, as it was eventually built, more closely resembled Cypress Gardens on steroids than any of the other Florida springs.

The attraction offered peaceful boat rides through tranquil canals and gardens, as well as not-so-peaceful "jumping boats" that performed dangerous stunts reminiscent of Cypress Gardens' water-ski shows. Oh, and Sunshine Springs had its own genuine water-ski shows too, complete with a skiing elephant that no doubt worked for peanuts. The Miss Florida pageant was held there as long as the attraction lasted, and Stuckey's thought the place had enough sticking power to set up one of its ubiquitous candy shops. Even a 315-foot observation tower was added. But the sun set on Sunshine Springs within just a few years of its opening. By 1960, the property had been sold for real estate development, and Florida's only known fake springs attraction was forgotten by even the water-skiing elephant.

Bonita Springs was the home of the Everglades Wonder Gardens on U.S. 41, also known as the Tamiami Trail. Opened by the Piper family in 1937, the Wonder Gardens were kept as natural and unspoiled as possible. In fact, in their official brochure, Wilford and Lester Piper went on record with this statement of purpose:

The Sunshine Springs brochure did not even try to camouflage the attraction's intentional resemblance to others.

BILL AND LESTER PIPER'S

EVERGLADES
Wonder Gardens
BONITA SPRINGS, FLORIDA

AN ALL-FLORIDA EXHIBIT

23 MILES
SOUTH OF
FORT MYERS,
FLORIDA

ON THE
TAMIAMI
TRAIL
U. S. 41

The Everglades Wonder Gardens have been a popular stopover at Bonita Springs since 1937.

We present the Everglades Wonder Gardens without any particular training in showmanship or exploitation. Years of actual experience and contact with wildlife have given us an intimate knowledge of their habits which we wish to share with you. We have only a sincere desire to give the visitor a clear picture of the thrilling life, dangers, intrigue and constant struggle for existence that goes on in the depths of the impenetrable and fascinating Everglades.

The Wonder Gardens featured a menagerie of beasts that rivaled its cousin Homosassa Springs, farther up the Gulf Coast, and shared something else in common with its northern relatives as well. One of the Wonder Gardens' featured performers was Tom the bear, which had costarred in *The Yearling* when that classic story was filmed at Silver Springs. The attraction also promoted Jimmy the talking crow, along with scores of other animals not given human monikers.

Seemingly any town or community with "Springs" in its name had the potential of making something out of it. Ponce de Leon Springs enjoyed some minor development for tourists but did not progress much past the local swimming-hole concept. Tarpon Springs, on U.S. 19 just north of Tampa, soaked up tourist dollars by promoting its connection with the sponge trade, although it also featured the peaceful Spring Bayou in its downtown area. On U.S. 41 south of Sarasota, you could heat things up at Warm Mineral Springs, with its eighty-seven-degree waters promoted as a cure for whatever ailed you. Other cities, towns, and wide spots in the road that named themselves after local springs included Altamonte Springs, Bay Springs, Bluff Springs, Citrus Springs, Coral Springs, Crystal Springs, DeFuniak Springs, Fort Green Springs, Green Cove Springs, Hampton Springs, High Springs, Miami Springs, Orange Springs, Salt Springs, Sarasota Springs, Suwannee Springs, Wekiva Springs, Winter Springs, and Zolfo Springs. Ask Florida natives about the springs phenomenon, and they will readily reel off any of these names as their favorite picnic or swimming spots.

T.S. 7—Beautiful Spring Bayou, "The Venice of the South," Tarpon Springs, Fla., U. S. A.

Tarpon Springs' tourism industry had two distinctly different sides: the grungy sponge-fishing sector and the elegant Spring Bayou in the downtown area.

It took a bit more ingenuity, money, creativity, and sometimes good old-fashioned hucksterism to turn a natural spring into a tourist attraction. That was the secret of the whole southern tourism industry, which prided itself on presenting sights that could not be seen elsewhere. Florida's glass bottom boats, performing mermaids, and animal movie and television stars might not have had the roadside all to themselves, but they certainly created ripples in their springs that extended far beyond the confinements of their banks.

BIBLIOGRAPHY

Books

Breslauer, Ken. *Roadside Paradise*. St. Petersburg, FL: Retro-Florida, 2000.

Browning, Ricou, ed. *Underwater Monkey Business*. Jacksonville, FL: H. and W. B. Drew Company, 1957.

Butko, Brian. *Roadside Giants*. Mechanicsburg, PA: Stackpole Books, 2005.

Corse, Carita Doggett. *Shrine of the Water Gods*. Silver Springs, FL: Ray and Davidson, 1947.

Dinkins, J. Lester. *Dunnellon: Boomtown of the 1890s*. St. Petersburg, FL: Great Outdoors Publishing, 1969.

Dyer, Rod. *Coast to Coast: The Best of Travel Decal Art*. New York: Abbeville, 1991.

Essoe, Gabe. *Tarzan of the Movies*. New York: Citadel Press, 1968.

Flynn, Stephen J. *Florida: Land of Fortune*. Washington, DC: Luce, 1962.

Fury, David. *Kings of the Jungle: An Illustrated Reference to Tarzan on Screen and Television*. Jefferson, NC: McFarland and Company, 1994.

Futrell, Jim. *Amusement Parks of Pennsylvania*. Mechanicsburg, PA: Stackpole Books, 2002.

Hollis, Tim. *Dixie before Disney: 100 Years of Roadside Fun*. Jackson, MS: University Press of Mississippi, 1999.

———. *Florida's Miracle Strip: From Redneck Riviera to Emerald Coast*. Jackson, MS: University Press of Mississippi, 2004.

———. "See Rock City: The Story of Rock City Gardens atop Lookout Mountain." Unpublished manuscript, 1992.

Kirby, Doug, with Ken Smith and Mike Wilkins. *The New Roadside America*. New York: Simon and Schuster, 1992.

Margolies, John. *Fun along the Road: American Tourist Attractions*. Boston: Little, Brown and Company, 1998.

Martin, Richard A. *Eternal Spring*. St. Petersburg, FL: Great Outdoors Publishing, 1966.

McCarthy, Kevin, and Ernest Jernigan. *Images of America: Ocala*. Charleston, SC: Arcadia Publishing, 2001.

McDowell, Frank E., Jr. *The Story of Six Gun Territory*. Ocala, FL: Six Gun Territory, 1965.

Riley, Ruth J. *Memories of Rainbow Springs*. Dunnellon, FL: Fruit Tree Press, 2000.

Newspaper and Magazine Articles

"Actor Lemmon Films 'Airport' at Wakulla." United Press International story, syndicated November 21, 1976.

Anderson, Odie. "Ft. Dodge—Fla.'s Newest Tourist Lure." *Variety,* undated clipping in Paul Bolstein collection.

"Area to Get Big Tourist Attraction." *Pensacola Journal,* June 22, 1962.

Ayers, Judith. "His Wild West Is in Florida." *Staten Island Advance,* August 27, 1965.

Belleville, Bill. "Florida's Beautiful and Exotic Springs." *Florida Trend,* July 1978.

Blyth, Ann. "Or Would You Rather Be a Fish?" Unidentified clipping in Delee Perry collection.

Burt, Al. "Ed Ball's Private Zoo Still Place of Beauty." *Miami Herald,* February 24, 1974.

Covington, Richard. "A Creature Feature." *Miami Magazine,* August 1979.

Crussell, Bud. "Newt Perry: Tarzan to Tierney." Unidentified clipping in Wakulla Springs collection, July 1, 1979.

Dickinson, Joy Wallace. "Mermaid-Filled Springs Show Has a Deep Past." *Orlando Sentinel,* August 17, 2003.

DuFoe, Terry, and Becky Dufoe. "Ricou Browning, the Creature from the Black Lagoon." *Planet X Magazine*, 1998.

Edger, Betsy. "Movie Stunts No Secret to Local Diver." *Ocala Star-Banner*, January 2, 1977.

"Fire at Wakulla Springs Hotel." Associated Press story, syndicated February 24, 1943.

Flanagan, Katie. "Synchronized Swimmers Take Two." *FSView*, June 2, 2003.

Gramling, Homer. "Florida's Newt Perry." *Miami Herald*, undated clipping in Delee Perry collection.

Harrell, Bob. "Old Bullochville Has Old Georgia Flavor." *Atlanta Constitution*, September 13, 1971.

"Homosassa in Filmland Focus." Unidentified clipping in Homosassa Springs collection.

Jubera, Drew. "Mermaids May Get Beached." *Atlanta Journal-Constitution*, July 27, 2003.

King, Wendy Adams. "Through the Looking Glass of Silver Springs: Tourism and the Politics of Vision." *Americana: The Journal of American Popular Culture*, Spring 2004.

Martinez, Bob. "Attractions and Oddities." *Old Brooksville in Photos and Stories*, January 2003.

Meiklejohn, Don. "Wakulla Springs May Be Disneyland, Fla." Unidentified clipping in Wakulla Springs collection, August 1959.

"Movie Scenes Shot at Wakulla Springs." *Tallahassee Democrat*, September 5, 1965.

O'Brien, Claudia. "The Wild, Wild West." *Ocala Style*, October 2004.

Phillips, Lynn. "Parent Company Plans to Sell Six Gun Territory." *Orlando Sentinel*, September 13, 1978.

Rizzo, Marian. "Tourist Season." *Ocala Star-Banner*, June 18, 1999.

Ross, Jim. "Past Park Manager Garner Dies at 62." *St. Petersburg Times*, May 2, 2000.

Ruth, Daniel. "It Isn't Easy to Finance Films in Florida." *Tampa Tribune*, July 27, 1977.

"See Florida from Orlando—Soon, Disneyland!" *Orlando Sentinel*, November 25, 1965.

Sherer, Ed. "Plans Revealed for 'Frontier Town' Attraction on Silver Springs Blvd." *Ocala Star-Banner*, May 24, 1962.

Skidmore, Sarah. "Weeki Wachee's Dance to Stay Afloat." *Florida Times-Union*, October 6, 2003.

Smith, Todd. "Fate of Nature World Attraction Hangs in Balance." Unidentified clipping in Homosassa Springs collection, August 3, 1986.

Stevenson, Franklin. "New Springs Developed." *Orlando Sentinel-Star,* undated clipping in Delee Perry collection.

Stinson, Lashonda. "Paradise Found." *Ocala Star-Banner,* February 28, 2005.

"Superb Attractions Don't Attract." *Tallahassee Democrat,* March 3, 1963.

Terrell, Bob. "R. B. Coburn: Mountaintop Disney." *Carolina Senior Citizen,* November 1991.

Wachendorf, George. "Have They Really Beaten Ed Ball?" *Florida Times-Union,* July 10, 1966.

"Walt Disney Film Made at Homosassa Springs." Unidentified clipping in Homosassa Springs collection.

Witwer, Stan. "Starvation Junction." *St. Petersburg Times,* September 17, 1967.

Wright, Mike. "Nature Attraction Poised for Change." *Citrus County Chronicle,* December 30, 1988.

Television and Video Productions

Greetings from Forgotten Florida. New River Media, 2000.

The Wonders of Wakulla Springs. Rich Kern's Nature Series, n.d.

Personal Interviews and Correspondence

Paul Bolstein, Lois Brauckmuller, Ken Breslauer, Ricou Browning, Kitty Carr Carpenter, David Cook, Ed Darlington, Tom Diehl, Susan Dougherty, Mary Darlington Fletcher, Neal Frisbie, Bonnie Georgiadis, Ginger Stanley Hallowell, Herbert Hooker, Ernest Jernigan, Charlene Johnson, Don Koppler, Jim Love, Doris Magusky, Robert Martinez, Diana Mitchell, Ted Newhall, Claudia O'Brien, Delee Perry, Bill Ray, Page Robinson, Joe Ryan, Vicki Smith, Steve Specht, Val Valentine, David Warren, Barbara Wynns, Genie Young.

INDEX

Page numbers in **bold** refer to illustrations

ABC–Paramount, **29**, **30**, 31–33, 45, 47,
   71, 102, 105, 113, 115, 116, 117
Adams, Dee Dee, 20, **21**
Adams, Julia, 22, 69
Airport '77, 73
Alice in Waterland, 103, **104**
Allen, Ross, 11–12, 13, 14, 28, 30, 85, 105
Altamonte Springs, Florida, 142
American Precision Industries, **45**, 46
Amphibious Warfare, 66–67
Animal Actors' Training Studio, 132
Aquarena Springs, 101
Around the World Under the Sea, 73
At Weeki Wachee, 114–15
Aunt Silla, 12–13, 27, 114

Ball, Edward, 60–61, 66, 68, 69, 71, 73–74, 75
Ball, Lucille, 12
Ballad of Silver Springs, The, 114
Bartlett, Tommy, 22–24, **25**, 33
Bay Springs, Florida, 142
Believe It Or Not, 11
Beverly Hillbillies, The, **54**, 55
Bienecke, Walter, 84–85, 86
Billy Rose Aquacade, 102
Bingham, Jackie, **17**

Birmingham, Alabama, 2
Blocker, Dan, 55
Blue Bird Restaurant, 38
Blue Run, 76
Blue Springs, 75–76, 77
Bluff Springs, Florida, 142
Blyth, Ann, 98–99, 117
Bolstein, Paul, **111**, 112–13
Bonanza, 55
Bonita Springs, Florida, 141–42
Boston, Massachusetts, 140
Boyetts Grove, 112
Bozo the Clown, **115**
Brahma Restaurant, 39, **40**
Branson, Missouri, 46
Breakfast with the Neptunes, 100
Bridal Chamber, 12–14, 27
Bridges, Beau, 117
Bridges, Lloyd, 30, 73, 117, 130
Brooksville, Florida, 93, 110, 130
Browning, Ricou, 20–21, 30–31, 68–69,
    130, 131
Buccaneer Bay, 117
Busch Gardens, 130
Byers, Clark, 81

Camp Blanding, 78
Camp Gordon Johnson, 66
Candle Glow Inn, 38
Carmichael, Ed, 8, 14
Carr, Kitty, **33**
Carrabelle, Florida, 66
Carriage Cavalcade, 41–43
Carter, Garnet, 36, 135
Cavalcadia
    See also Carriage Cavalcade

CBS, 22, 33
Chaney, Marx, 136
Chase Ventures, 88
Chattanooga, Tennessee, 36
Cherokee, North Carolina, 54
Chicago, Illinois, 122
Christus Gardens, 25
Citrus County, Florida, 133
Citrus Springs, Florida, 142
Civil War, 7
Clarence the Cross-Eyed Lion, 130,
    131, 132
Coburn, R. B., 46–47, 54, 56, 58, 112
Cody, Buffalo Bill, 47
Colorado Springs, Colorado, 116
Congo Belle, 105
Cooper, Gary, 20
Coral Springs, Florida, 142
Cordrey's Tourist Court, 37
Corley, Bob, 28–29
Corse, Carita Doggett, 6, 10
Cowboy in Africa, A, 131
Creature from the Black Lagoon, The,
    20, 21–22, 30–31, 68–69
Creature Walks Among Us, The, 22
Crow's Nest Restaurant, **125**
Crystal Springs, Florida, 142
Cunningham, Paul, 25–26, 33
Cypress Gardens, 22, 72, 140, 141

Daktari, 131
Darlington, Ed, 93, **94**
Darlington, Mary, 93, **94**
Davidson, "Shorty", 8–9, 10, 36
Day, Doris, 31
DeFuniak Springs, Florida, 142
Digger the undertaker, 52
Disney, Walt, 71, 116, 129–30, 139
Disneyland, 46, 71
Distant Drums, 20
Dixie Before Disney, 1
Dixie Highway, 81, 110–11
Douglass, Claire, 12–14, 114
Dunnellon, Florida, 75, 78, 81, 83, 86
Dunnellon State Bank, 86
DuPont, Alfred, 60, 73

Early American Museum, 43–45
Ebsen, Buddy, **54**, 55
Edwards, Dave, 79–80, **80**, 89
1890 Beef House, 38

Eisenhower, Dwight, 81
Eternal Spring, 7
Everglades Wonder Gardens, 141–42

Fanning Springs, Florida, 136–38
Field and Stream, 121
Fleischer, Max, 23
Flipper, 130
Florida Attractions Association, 88, **107**
Florida Citrus Commission, **50**
Florida East Coast Railroad, 60
Florida Folk Festival, 139
Florida Highway 40, 35, 37, 39, 46, **48**, 55, 58
Florida Highway 471, 108
Florida Leisure Attractions, 33, 116
Florida National Bank, 60
Florida Pictorial, 113, **114**
Florida Reptile Institute, 11–12, 14, 105
Florida State College for Women, **66**, 67
Florida State University, 67
Florida's Miracle Strip, 1
Floridaland, 140
Forest Flite, **84**, 85, 89
Fort Dodge, **111**, 112–13
Fort Green Springs, Florida, 142
Fort Moultrie, South Carolina, 86
Foxbower Wildlife Museum, 109
Frazee, Betty, **29**
Frontier City, 46
Frontier Land, 54, 56

Gainesville, Florida, 78
Garner, James, 102
Gatlinburg, Tennessee, 25
Gentle Ben, 131, 132, 134
Gentle Giant, 131

Georgiadis, Bonnie, 103
Ghost Town in the Glen, 57
Ghost Town in the Sky, 47, 56, 58
Glass Bottom Boat, The, 31
Glenn Springs, Florida, 100
Gog, 130
Gold Nugget Junction, 113
Great Depression, 60, 75, 91
Great Smoky Mountains, 81
Green Cove Springs, Florida, 142
Greene, Frank, 75
Griffith, Andy, 29
Gunsmoke, 58

Hallowell, Ginger Stanley, 19–21, 22, 69, 125
Hampton Springs, Florida, 142
Hawkes, Steve, 85
Head, Sheila, 124
Hello Down There, 131
Hemphill, F.E., 75, 77
Hemphill, John, 75, 77
Henry the Pole-Vaulting Fish, 61, 74
Herwede, Mr., 108–09
High Springs, Florida, 142
Hines, Duncan, 79
Holiday Inn, **27**, 37, **39**, 41, 46, 86–87, 88, 106, **109**
Homosassa, Florida., 119
Homosassa Springs, 73, 105, 119–34, 135, 137, 142
Hooker, Herbert, 58
Hope, Bob, 102
Horne's, 39
Hot Springs, Arkansas, 23
Howard Johnson's, 39
Hunting and Fishing Club of the Air, 120
Hutchins, Will, 102

I-75, 33, 81–82, 83, 84, 87, 113, 115–16, 132, 137–38, 139
I. Q. Zoo, 23

Incredible Mr. Limpet, The, 103–04
International Deer Ranch, 3, **22**, 23–24, 28, 30, 33, 43, 47
Island of the Lost, 131

Jarvis Oil Company, 41
Jarvis, Sam and Vernon, 41, 45
Jefferson, Lauretta, 102–03
Jimmy the crow, 142
Jones, Hullam, 9–10, 31
Judy the chimp, **131**, 132, 134
Jungle Cruise, 15–16, 33–34, 61
Junior Museum, 72
Jupiter's Darling, 20–21

Kelly, Karol, 124
Killearn Gardens State Park, 72
Knott's Berry Farm, 46
Knotts, Don, 103–04, **106**

Lake of the Ozarks, Missouri, 113
Lanier, Sidney, 7
Legend of El Blanco, The, 129–30
Lemmon, Jack, 73
Lewis, Pearce, 110–11
Lewis Plantation, 110–11
Lockett, Manning, 78–79
Longwood, Florida, 136
Lookout Mountain, 36, 81
Los Angeles, California, 14
Lucifer the hippopotamus, 132, 133–34
Lyon, H., 114

Mack, Ted, 102
Macon, Georgia, 28
Maggie Valley, North Carolina, 46, 58
Magnetic Monster, The, 130
Mansfield, Jayne, 22
Marineland, 22, 72
Marlin and the Mermaids, 113–14
Martin, Richard A., 7, 10, 16
Maximum Bob, 117
May Tropical Exhibit, 105, **107**, 116
Mayo, Bernice, 12–14, 114
McGrath, Frank, **54**, 55
McLean, Will, 114
Meiklejohn, Don, 71
Memphis, Tennessee, 86
Mermaid Motel, 106
Mermaid Village, 103
MGM, 14–15, 64–66

Miami, Florida, 23, 73, 81, 86, 98, 130
Miami Springs, Florida, 142
Miss Florida Pageant, 141
Mississippi River, 110
Mr. Peabody and the Mermaid, 98–100
Monkey Jungle, 130
Morrell, Phillip, 9–10, 31
Mozert, Bruce, 19–20, 125
Myers, Teresa, 94
Mystery Mountain, 113

National Service Industries (NSI), 56–58
Nature World, 133
Nature's Giant Fish Bowl, 120–22
Nemours Foundation, 73
Neptune's Holiday Inn, 106
Neptune's Scholars, 14
Newell, David, 120–21, 125, 134
Nixon, Richard, 87
Norris, Bruce, 122, 124, 125, 130, 131–32, 134
Number One Street, 28–29

Oakley, Annie, 47
Ocala, Florida 8, 14, 19, 20, 29, 35, 46, 47, 58, 59, 61, 72, 75, 101, 135
Ocala Star-Banner, 88
Ocali, 6
Ocklawaha River, 7, 8, 89
Okefenokee Swamp, 129
Oklahoma City, Oklahoma, 46
Old Bullochville, 113
Old Salty Mine, **111**, 113
Oliver, Marilyn, **131**
OPEC, 87
Orange Springs, Florida, 142
Orangeburg, South Carolina, 46
Orlando, Florida, 33, 87, 129, 136
Osceola, 86

Palm Beach, Florida, 56
Palmetto Leaves, 7
Panama City Beach, Florida, 113
Paradise Park, **26**, 27–28
Pearson, Russell, 46–47, 51–52, 54
Pensacola, Florida, 60
Pensacola Journal, 71
Perry, Delee, 14, **32**, 92
Perry, Newton, 14–15, 19, **32**, 62–65, 67–68, 92–95, 97–101, 102, 110, 118

Petticoat Junction, 113
Philadelphia, Pennsylvania, 87
Piper, Wilford and Lester, 141
Plantation Pancake Inn, 38–39
Ponce de Leon Springs, 142
Powell, William, 98
Presley, Elvis, **106**
Prince of Peace Memorial, 25–26,
    28, 33

Rainbow Cottages, **82**
Rainbow Falls, 78
Rainbow Lodge, 79, **80**, 81
Rainbow Queen, 77–78, 79, 85, 88, 89
Rainbow River, 76, 77
Rainbow Springs, **2**, 75–90, 115, 121,
    135
Ramada Inn, 39
Ray, Bill, 8, 10–11, 16–17, 18–19, 30
Ray, Carl, Jr., 31
Ray and Davidson, 9, 10, 14, 15, 17, 27,
    29, 31, 33, 36, 47, 59, 75, 136
Ray, William Carl, 8–9, 10, 11
Revenge of the Creature, 22
Rice, Grantland, 14, 63, 66–67, 97, 100
Ripley, Robert, 11–12, 13
Riverside Villas, 132
Robinson, Page, 54, 56
Rock, Alan, **115**
Rock City, 29–30, 36, 81, 135
Rocky Glen Park, 57
Rogers Christmas House, 111–12
Rogers, Will, 47
Route 66, 3
Russell, Jane, 22
Ryan, Irene, 55
Ryan, Joe, 87

St. Augustine, Florida, 22, 60
St. Joe Paper Company, 60
St. Petersburg, Florida, 92, 113
St. Petersburg Times, 82, 137–38
Salt Springs, Florida, 142
San Marcos, Texas, 101
Sanford, Florida, 136
Sanlando Springs, **135**, 136
Sarasota, Florida, 139, 142
Sarasota Springs, Florida, 142
Science Fiction Theater, 130
Scranton, Pennsylvania, 57
Sea Hunt, 30–31, 73, 130

Seminole Village, 11, **12**, 86, 105,
    106, 116
S&H Green Stamps, 84, 88
Shakespeare, William, 13
Shalimar Motor Court, 37, **39**, 41
Shoppes at Silver Springs, 58
Shrine of the Water Gods, 6
Shriver, Otis, 86
Silver Dollar City, 46
Silver River, 15
Silver Springs, 3, 4, 5–34, 35–37, 41–42,
    45, 47, 59, 61, 62, 63, 69, 72, 73, 75,
    85, 86, 92, 105, 113–14, 117, 121,
    125, 130, 135, 142
Silver Springs Boulevard, 35
Silver Springs Railroad, 39–40, 55
Sinclair, 109–10
Six Gun Plaza, 58
Six Gun Territory, **3**, 46–58, 112, 113
Smith, Hall, 92, 93
Southwest Florida Water Management
    District, 116
Spider-Man, 55
Sportlights, 14, 63, **64**
Spring Bayou, 142, **143**
Spring Side Motel, 37
Stackpole Books, 3
Stage Stop Restaurant, 55
Standard Oil, **27**
Star Garden, 103, **105**, 118
Stephen Foster Memorial, 138–39
Stowe, Harriet Beecher, 7
Stuckey's, 39, 141
Sun Plaza Motel, 37, **38**
Sunshine Springs, **139**, 140–41
Sunshine State, 117
Suwannee Gables Motel, 138

Uncle Tom, 7
Underwater!, 22
Underwater Circus, 14
Underwater Romance, 14
Universal Studios, 68–69, 98–99
University Press of Mississippi, 1

Valentine, Val, 23–24, **25**, 39–43, **127**
Veterans of Foreign Wars (VFW), **44**, 45
Von Braun, Wernher, 102

Wagon Train, **54**, 55
Wahoo Bobcat, The, 129
Wakulla Springs, 2, 14, 15, 22, 59–74,
    75, 85, 92, 94, 117, 121, 135
Walt Disney World, 33, 87, 116, 132
Warm Mineral Springs, 142
Warm Springs, Georgia, 113
Warner Brothers, 103
Warner, Suzanne, 124
Washington, D.C., 26
Wayne, John, 58
Weaver, Kyle, 3
Weekend at Weeki Wachee, 104–05
Weeki Wachee Spring, 14, 19, 31, 33,
    63–64, 67, 68, 69, 71, 83, 91–118,
    135, 137
Weissmuller, Johnny, 14–15, 20, **65**
Wekiva Springs, Florida, 142
Western Heritage USA, 46
What a Picnic!, 63
What it Was Was Football, 29
White Springs, Florida, 138–39
Wilderness Chief Covered Wagon,
    105–06, **108**
Williams, Esther, 20–21
Willow Grove Park, 57
Winona, 14
Winter Springs, Florida, 142
Wisconsin Dells, 22–23
Wizard of Oz, The, 103, **104**
Wonderful World of Color, 129–30
World War I, 8
World War II, 16–17, 36, 66–67, 78, 91,
    92, 136

Yearling, The, 20, 142

Zebra in the Kitchen, 131
Zolfo Springs, Florida, 142

Suwannee River, 136, 138
Suwannee River Jungle Drive, 136–38
Suwannee Springs, Florida, 142
Swim-In Court, 37

Tallahassee Democrat, 72
Tallahassee, Florida, 22, 60, 67, 71,
    72, 115
Talmadge, Grace, 87
Talmadge Tours, 87
Tamiami Trail, 141
Tampa, Florida, 14, **98**, 99, 115, 142
Tanner, Leonard, 140
Tarpon Club, **66**, 67–68
Tarpon Springs, Florida, 93, 142, **143**
Tarzan, 14–15, 16, 20, 64–66, 68, 85
Tarzan, the Brown Prince, 85
Tarzan Finds a Son, 15, 64–65
Tarzan's New York Adventure, 66
Tarzan's Secret Treasure, 65
Timuqua, 6
Tom the bear, 142
Tooey, Colonel, 15–16, 61
Toonerville Trolley, 42–43
Tors, Ivan, 30, 73, 130–32, 133, 134
Travelodge, 39
Tribble, Nancy, 94, **98**, 99, 100

U.S. 1, 28
U.S. 19, 82, 83, 106, 109, 112, 113, 115,
    136–37, 142
U.S. 27, 82
U.S. 41, 81–82, 83, 85, 110, 115, 138–39,
    141, 142
U.S. 441, 82